HOMEMADE MEALS

HOMEMADE MEALS

Caroline Barty

Bridget Jones

Liz Wolf-Cohen

Photography by Ian Garlick

MQP

An Hachette Livre UK Company
First published in Great Britain in 2006 by MQ Publications,
a division of Octopus Publishing Group Ltd
2–4 Heron Quays
London E14 4JP

www.octopusbooks.co.uk

Copyright © Octopus Publishing Group Ltd 2006, 2008
Recipes: Caroline Barty, Bridget Jones, Liz Wolf-Cohen
Photography: Ian Garlick
Home Economy: Felicity Barnum-Bobb
Illustrations: Penny Brown

ISBN 978-1-84601-095-8

Printed and bound in China

10 9 8 7 6 5 4 3 2

This book contains the opinions and ideas of the author. It is intended to
provide helpful and informative material on the subjects addressed in this book
and is sold with the understanding that the authors and publisher are not
engaged in rendering any kind of personal professional services in this book.
The authors and publisher disclaim all responsibility for any liability, loss or
risk, personal or otherwise, which is incurred as a consequence, directly or
indirectly, of the use and application of any of the contents of this book.

IMPORTANT: Those who might be at risk from the effects of salmonella
poisoning (the elderly, pregnant women, young children and
those suffering from immune deficiency diseases) should consult
their GP with any concerns about eating raw eggs.

Contents

Introduction

Surrounded by fast food outlets, meals on the run and off-the-shelf pre-cooked meals, the mention of 'homemade' when referring to food conjures up the image of a dish that is nutritious, freshly made with quality ingredients, by hand, and not delivered off a factory conveyor belt.

Think back to the time of your grandmother when all meals were 'homemade'. In just a few decades our eating habits have been turned on their head and we have become dependent on convenience foods and burger bars. In our eagerness to pack more into our lives, and for families where both parents work, the desire to give up less time to cooking has become the norm and made us dependent on convenience foods. Needless to say, we relish the taste of 'homemade' food, as when we have been invited to a meal where the table is groaning with a crispy roast chicken, hand-cut fries and a melt-in-the-mouth Angel cake.

The exponential rise of ready-prepared meals on our supermarket shelves means that we are cooking less and less and losing basic cooking skills. This in turn makes us hesitant, insecure cooks who will scurry off to pick up a takeout or add a jar of ready-made ragù to a plate of spaghetti rather than struggle to make a dish that may or may not work out. We are opting for the convenience of having a meal that requires no more effort than switching on the oven or moving a package from the freezer to the microwave. There is a great deal to be said for the speed in which a meal can be served up – there are occasions when it is the perfect solution to a long day or to the unexpected arrival of four extra teenage mouths to fill, or to a sports fixture on the television that cannot be interrupted. But we all know that it never tastes as good as when you make it yourself, and that most often it contains more salt, sugar and flavour enhancers than is good for us.

Homemade Meals shows us that cooking doesn't have to be a chore, that it needn't take a lifetime to prepare, and that we don't have to be a superchef to make a tasty, wholesome dish. Remember too, that homemade meals do not have to look as if they have been restaurant made. That's not homemade. A dish can look a little rough around the edges and still be tasty. Homemade is going for second helpings!

Each recipe in the first four chapters of this book is part of a menu. On each recipe you will find a menu suggestion. So if you fancy a Tuna Noodle Casserole then you can complete the meal with the rest of the dishes on the menu. For quick reference you can consult the Menu Ideas on page 248. The menus are a guideline only, offering a balance of daily food requirements, tastes and textures, and time management. Choose the main dish as your starting point and then consider dishes that will complement and highlight individual qualities of the different ingredients. Use your personal preferences as a guide.

Equipment

KNIVES & OTHER CUTTING EQUIPMENT

A good sharp knife that is comfortable to hold is the most essential tool in the kitchen. There is nothing worse than having to hack vegetables and saw your way through meat. Knives should be kept razor sharp. To help preserve their cutting edge, always chop on a wooden board or plastic board. Do not store your knives in cutlery drawer – the edges get dulled and it is dangerous when someone reaches in. Keep them slotted individually in a wooden knife block.

Chopping knife

To chop vegetables and herbs you will need a well-balanced, general purpose cook's knife that tapers to a pointed tip.

Knife for slicing

For slicing bread you will need a knife with a long blade with hollow-ground serrations; for slicing cold meats use a knife with a long and narrow blade with good flexibility; for slicing fruit and vegetables use a small serrated knife.

Paring & peeling knife

Use these to peel and slice your vegetables. The blade of a paring knife should always be sharp.

Carving knife

This has a long, narrow blade for slicing hot, cooked meats, and is often used with a double-pronged fork to keep the meat steady.

Meat-boning knife

This knife has a curved blade and a sharp end which can tunnel through meat easily. It's not suitable for any other job.

Filleting knife

This is the only knife to use when you have a fish to fillet. Its long, flexible blade is perfectly equipped to separate delicate flesh from bones.

Poultry shears

These heavy-duty scissors, which have one serrated blade, can easily cut through bone and cartilage.

Grater

Choose a box-shaped or conical grater that will sit squarely on a board without shifting as you grate. Each side should have a different grating surface so you can grate a variety of food textures from soft (cheese) to very hard (nutmeg).

OTHER EQUIPMENT

Pans

A set of three or four saucepans is probably sufficient for most households. The size of your pans depends on how many people on average you are catering for. Buy pans that have a thick and heavy gauge metal on the bottom with lids that give a tight seal. Handles should be strong and comfortable to hold and preferably heat insulated. Non-stick surfaces are fabulous for heating milk and cooking eggs and fish where almost no fat is required for cooking.

Wok

This is a very inexpensive and versatile addition to your kitchen equipment. The most useful wok that comes with a fitting lid is 35cm in diameter. After cooking, wash the wok with hot soapy water and a brush and dry thoroughly, then momentarily place it over a hot flame. To prevent rusting, lightly wipe the inside with a little vegetable oil.

Frying pans & griddle pans

Choose a thick-based, non-stick frying pan for even cooking. A griddle pan is useful for searing meat, fish and vegetables – the best griddle pans have deep ridges so that the meat can sit above its fat.

Roasting tins

Stainless steel roasting tins are probably the best. Heavier ones will not scorch on the bottom when placed on the top of the stove. Select one that best fits the contours of your oven. Similarly, make sure the pan is the correct size for the quantities in which you usually cook. The sides should be low enough for heat to access the surface of the food, but deep enough to hold rendered fats and juices. A rack may be placed at the bottom of the pan, allowing for even roasting and for juices and fat to drip away.

Casserole dishes

Enamelled cast iron and clad metal casseroles are best because they conduct heat evenly. Make sure you have one with a tight-fitting lid.

Garlic press

Choose a sturdy aluminium or stainless steel press with a coarse mesh. Remember, crushed garlic from a press is more potent in flavour than chopped garlic. The good thing about a press is that you don't have to peel the garlic segments.

Pestle & mortar

If you want to crush herbs and spices to release their rich aromas, a solid, heavy pestle and mortar do the best job.

Sieves & colanders

Round-framed stainless steel sieves are preferable to the wire or plastic mesh variety. Stainless steel does not stain or corrode. Colanders are particularly useful for draining pasta and vegetables.

BOARDS

A big, solid wooden chopping board is your kitchen's best friend. Make sure you keep your board scrupulously clean, washing thoroughly with

detergent between ingredients to avoid cross-contamination. Buy the best board you can afford and it'll last for years. If you are particularly concerned about hygiene, you could have colour-coded plastic chopping boards. Keep green for chopping vegetables, red for meat, blue for fish and the others for cooked foods. A mezzaluna or 'half moon' implement makes chopping herbs a breeze. Simply rock the blade to and for across the special curved chopping board.

WHISKS
Twirl whisk
This manual whisk is flexible and useful for working around the entire base of the bowl or pan. Great for preventing lumps.
Spiral whisk
This is ideal for whisking sauces in shallow dishes and for getting into the corners of the bowl.
Egg whisk
This has more wires than an ordinary balloon whisk making it good for aerating egg-based sauces and egg whites for meringue.
Balloon whisk
The classic whisk can be used for aerating both light and heavy ingredients. It's especially good for cream and butter sauces.

BOWLS
Ceramic bowl
A traditional bowl finished with a white glaze is comfortable and easy to handle.
Copper bowl
A non-reactive copper bowl makes your meringue more stable and easier to work with.
Glass bowl
This is a good general mixing bowl, suitable for all ingredients and heavy enough to sit firmly on the work top.
Melamine bowl
Practical, cheap and unbreakable, plastic-based bowls often have a non-slip rubber base.
Stainless steel bowl
Stainless steel is ideal for all food preparation as it is resistant to food acids and colours.

BLENDERS & FOOD PROCESSORS
Food processors are extremely versatile – they can chop, mince purée, shred and slice many ingredients. Blenders are good for liquefying food to make soups, sauces and purées.

MEASURING CUPS/SPOONS
Level off ingredients in the spoons or cups for accuracy.

Staples

We are all too familiar with cupboards full of items that have been there for several years. Clear out anything that has been open for more than six months – many items should be tossed within just weeks of opening. If you are cooking for few, buy little. It may appear to be uneconomical to purchase small amounts but it is just the other side of the coin to throw away larger quantities that have been cheaper buys.

Fresh over frozen

Whenever possible buy fresh and in season and if you can, try to buy local. That way you will be able to savour new season tastes and choose recipes that reflect the passing months.

GRAINS, PULSES & PASTA

Grains

Grains are the edible seeds of grasses. Whether you are shopping for barley, bulghur wheat, maize, oatmeal or wheat, make sure you buy it fresh. The grain should be dry plump, and even in colour.

- *Wheat*
- *Oats*
- *Barley*
- *Corn*
- *Basmati rice*
- *Arborio rice*
- *American long-grain rice*
- *Brown rice*
- *Wild rice*
- *Couscous*
- *Polenta*

Pulses

Beans and pulses are extremely nutritious. They are low in fat and sodium and high in fibre.

- *Red split lentils*
- *Green and brown lentils*
- *Puy lentils*
- *Haricot beans*
- *Cannellini beans*
- *Chickpeas*
- *Broad beans*
- *Black-eyed beans*

Pasta

Pasta can be made just with flour and water, or with eggs too. The best commercially bought pasta is marked '100% whole durum' or 'pure semolina' and comes from southern Italy. Different types of pasta suit different types of sauce – thick, creamy sauces are best with chunky shapes such as penne or fusilli. Oil-based sauces suit fine pastas such as spaghetti, and chunky meat sauces are best cooked in lasagne or cannelloni. Asian noodles are mainly made from wheat, rice, buckwheat or mung beans. The most popular are rice noodles and egg noodles.

- *Spaghetti*
- *Tagliatelle*
- *Macaroni*
- *Fusilli*
- *Farfalle*
- *Cannelloni*
- *Lasagne*

SEASONINGS

Salt

Keep a small bowl of coarse salt near the stove. Sea salt and kosher salt are highly favoured in cooking and flavouring because of the absence of additives and chemicals. Generally it is in the form of larger flakes or crystals so keep a special mill for grinding.

- *Sea salt*
- *Sel gris*
- *Kosher salt*
- *Common salt*
- *Iodized salt*
- *Rock salt*
- *Seasoned salt*

Pepper

Pepper is one of the most versatile spices – not only does it add its own distinctive flavouring, but it also helps to enhance other flavours. Chilli powder is a blended spice that may also contain paprika, cayenne, black pepper and salt.

- *Black peppercorn*
- *White peppercorn*
- *Green peppercorn*
- *Chilli powder*
- *Cayenne pepper*
- *Paprika*

Mustard

Mustard has been a popular condiment for thousands of years. The hot taste is released when crushed mustard seeds are mixed with liquid. English mustard is one of the hottest; Dijon is blended with wine or vinegar to give it its distinctive taste.

- *Dijon*
- *English*
- *American*
- *German*
- *Wholegrain*

Vinegar

Vinegar is a by-product of wine-making, hence the different varieties such as cider and wine vinegar. Balsamic vinegar is sweeter, richer and darker.

- *Wine vinegar*
- *Cider vinegar*
- *Malt vinegar*
- *Balsamic vinegar*
- *Flavoured vinegar*

Sauces & condiments

There are so many sauces and condiments you can buy that you should try to keep a variety of them in your storecupboard – that way you will always have one to complement any meal.

- *Tomato ketchup*
- *Tomato purée*
- *Chilli sauce*
- *Mayonnaise*
- *Redcurrant jelly*
- *Mint sauce*
- *Fruit preserve*
- *Chutney*

- *Fish sauce* is a strong, salty liquid, very popular in Southeast Asia.
- *Soy sauce* is one of the most important ingredients in Chinese cookery and comes in light and dark, the dark being the stronger, sweeter variety.
- *Worcestershire sauce* is made from, amongst others, tamarind, molasses, anchovies, soy sauce, onions sugar and lime.

Herbs

Five herbs which have delicate leaves and are best when they have just been picked are basil, chervil, mint, parsley and tarragon. They are at their optimum flavour raw. Robust herbs such as bay leaf, marjoram, oregano, rosemary, sage can withstand higher cooking temperature.

Bouquet garni is, at its simplest, parsley, thyme and bay leaf tied together with string, but can just be a bunch of herbs of your choice.

Fines herbes are a combination of fresh chervil, parsley, tarragon and chives.

- *Parsley*
- *Chives*
- *Tarragon*
- *Dill*
- *Fennel*
- *Coriander*
- *Basil*
- *Marjoram*
- *Oregano*
- *Rosemary*
- *Sage*
- *Bay*
- *Thyme*
- *Mint*

Spices

Buy in small quantities and whenever possible use whole spices. This is where your pestle and mortar comes in handy.

- *Clove*
- *Cinnamon*
- *Allspice*
- *Ginger*
- *Turmeric*
- *Saffron*
- *Vanilla*
- *Coriander*
- *Mace*

Nuts & seeds

Nuts are very nutritious, containing many vitamins and minerals, but are also high in fat. It is best to buy them still in their shell as they keep better this way. Keep nuts and seeds in an airtight container in a cool dark place.

- *Hazelnuts*
- *Pine nuts*
- *Cashew nuts*
- *Almonds (blanched, flaked and ground)*
- *Brazil nuts*
- *Walnuts*
- *Pecans*
- *Sesame seeds*
- *Sunflower seeds*
- *Poppy seeds*
- *Pumpkin seeds*

OILS

Unrefined oils are those that have been cold pressed and left to mature for a few months before bottling. They tend to be cloudy and flavoursome.

Refined oils have been extracted by modern mechanical methods. They have treated for extended shelf life and clarity.

Virgin olive oil is useful for salads and other dishes where the fruity flavour of the oil can be savoured. Mediterranean dishes benefit from the use of olive oil. Olive oil is not suitable for deep frying.

Groundnut oil is a good replacement for olive oil when used for frying as it has very little smell and no flavour that will interfere with the taste of the food being prepared.

Corn oil is one of the most economical oils for shallow and deep frying, having one of the highest smoke points.

Safflower oil is very light and is recommended for use in low-cholesterol diets.

Walnut oil is an excellent addition to salads especially spinach. It does not keep well and it is recommended to buy small quantities.

Vegetable oils are a blend of various vegetable products – soyabean, coconut, palm, cottonseed and rapeseed. They are good for frying because of their high smoke point.

Palm and coconut oil are high in saturated fats and should be avoided by those on low-cholesterol diets.

Flavoured oils are good in salad dressings. Make your own by adding herbs, spices and citrus zests to good olive oil and leaving it to steep for a month.

BAKING

Sugar

Natural brown sugars come from raw sugar cane that retain some of the flavour and goodness of the cane; white sugars contain no protein, vitamins or minerals. Molasses sugar is soft, strong-flavoured and very moist good for gingerbread, fudge and fruit cakes. Demerara sugar is gritty with large granules.

- *Granulated sugar*
- *Caster sugar*
- *Icing sugar*
- *Demerara sugar*
- *Golden syrup*
- *Corn syrup*
- *Molasses and black treacle*

Flour

The most-used flours are made from wheat, but there is also flour made of rice, rye, buckwheat, corn and potato. Keep flour in an airtight container in a cool, dark, dry place.

- *Plain flour*
- *Self-raising flour*
- *Bread flour*
- *Italian flour*
- *Wholemeal flour*
- *Cornflour*

Raising agents

Always keep the essential raising agents in your cupboard as they are used extensively in baking. Do check the date on easy-blend yeasts as they tend to have a short shelf life.

- *Easy-blend yeast*
- *Baking powder*
- *Bicarbonate of soda*

Fats

Useful for cooking and baking, butter is also the base of many sauces.

- *Salted butter*
- *Margarine*
- *Unsalted butter*
- *Shortening*

Cream & yoghurt

A thick, rich cream complements many a pie while yoghurt is particularly good added to cooked dishes.

- *Single cream*
- *Whipping Cream*
- *Crème fraîche*
- *Double cream*
- *Soured cream*
- *Natural yoghurt*

MISCELLANEOUS ITEMS

- *Stock cubes*
- *Raisins, currants and sultanas*
- *Garlic*
- *Honey*
- *Coconut cream*
- *Gelatine*
- *Dried mushrooms*
- *Olives*
- *Capers*

COOKING METHODS

You do not have to be a trained chef to turn out a tasty meal. Practice makes perfect, and the more dishes you try, the more confident you will become. If you are an absolute beginner choose the easy options – soups and casseroles which are hard to get wrong. Read the recipe carefully before you begin to ensure that you have all the necessary ingredients (ingredient substitutes midway through preparation are not advised until you feel that you are a secure cook who has an understanding of how ingredients function and interact with other ingredients).

A few points for a healthy & happy kitchen

Make your kitchen environment an enjoyable place to be in. Keep it clean and clutter free. It is extremely difficult to be a relaxed cook if you are constantly hunting lost or mislaid tools and ingredients. Try to be organized – have your ingredients measured out and to hand and follow the guidelines below to make your kitchen a safer place.

- Always wash your hands with soap before and after handling food. Rinse well.
- Keep cuts and grazes covered with a waterproof plaster.
- Always wash food. Soak fruit and vegetables for a few minutes in a bowl of clean water then rinse under a running tap.
- Wash raw poultry under running water and then pat dry with kitchen paper.
- Thoroughly clean all surfaces that have come in contact with raw poultry.
- Keep separate chopping boards for raw meat, fish, poultry and vegetables. Buy a set of coloured boards – red for meat, pink for poultry, blue for fish, green for vegetables. It makes life much simpler.
- Wash kitchen utensils between preparing raw and cooked foods.
- Keep tea-towels clean and change frequently.
- Once food is cooked do not leave unrefrigerated for too long and never cover cooling food.
- Never re-heat food more than once. Make sure that it is piping hot all the way through.
- Store perishable foods at the correct temperature.
- Keep all refrigerated food covered and wipe up spills immediately with kitchen paper.
- Store raw meat, poultry and fish at the bottom of the fridge so that blood or moisture does not drip on cooked food. This prevents bacterial cross-contamination.
- Thoroughly clean your fridge using a special germicidal fridge cleaner.

POULTRY

- Spiced Chicken Pilaf with Dried Fruit & Nuts
- Spicy Chicken Kebabs
- Stir-fried Chicken with Chilli & Sweet Basil
- Chicken Satay Skewers with Sweet Chilli Sauce
- Southern Fried Chicken
- Spicy Chicken Enchiladas
- Club Sandwiches
- Stuffed Cabbage Leaves
- Chicken Hunter-style
- Halloween Chicken
- Honey-orange Chicken
- Chicken Kiev
- Traditional Roast Chicken

- Grilled Spiced Chicken
- Chicken & Vegetable Pie
- Spicy Peanut Chicken Noodles
- Chicken Tikka
- Lemon Chicken with Herb Tagliatelle
- Spicy Chicken Sausages
- Apple & Ginger Turkey Sandwiches
- Roast Turkey with Sausage & Sage Stuffing
- Spicy Turkey Meatballs
- Turkey-stuffed Peppers

CHAPTER ONE

POULTRY

Spiced Chicken Pilaf
with Dried Fruit & Nuts

Serves 4

50g butter
6 green cardamom pods, lightly
   crushed
1 cinnamon stick
2 bay leaves
225g basmati rice
300ml chicken stock
1 tablespoon vegetable oil
1 medium onion, finely chopped
25g flaked almonds
25g pistachio nuts, shelled and roughly
   chopped
50g dried figs, roughly chopped
25g dried apricots, roughly chopped
175g boneless chicken breast, skinned
   and cut into chunks
3 tablespoons chopped fresh coriander
Salt and freshly ground black pepper

1 Melt half the butter in a saucepan or casserole with a tight-fitting lid. Add the cardamom pods and cinnamon stick and cook for about 30 seconds before adding the bay leaves and rice. Stir well to coat the rice in the butter and add the stock. Bring to the boil, cover tightly and reduce the heat to low. Cook very gently for 15 minutes. Remove from the heat and leave to stand for 5 minutes.

2 Heat the remaining butter and vegetable oil in a wok or frying pan. When hot, add the onion and nuts. Stir-fry for 3–4 minutes until the nuts are beginning to brown.

3 Reduce the heat slightly and add the figs, apricots and chicken and continue to stir-fry for a further 7–8 minutes, or until the chicken is cooked through.

4 Remove from the heat and add the hot cooked rice and chopped coriander. Stir together well. Season to taste and serve hot.

Menu

Spiced Chicken Pilaf
with Dried Fruit &
Nuts
~
Spinach with Paneer
(p.151)
~
Tropical Fruit Salad
(p.221)

Spicy Chicken Kebabs

Serves 4

4 skinless, boneless chicken breast
 fillets
2 tablespoons olive oil
1 tablespoon ground coriander
1 tablespoon ground cumin
1 teaspoon ground turmeric
1 teaspoon chilli powder
Salt and freshly ground black pepper
4 pitta breads
4 handfuls of shredded iceberg lettuce
2 tomatoes, sliced
1 small red onion, thinly sliced
Small handful of fresh coriander leaves

For the dressing
150g natural yoghurt
2 tablespoons chopped fresh mint

1 Soak 8 wooden skewers in water for 30 minutes. Cut the chicken breast fillets into large chunks and place in a bowl. Mix the oil, ground coriander, cumin, turmeric and chilli powder together in a large bowl, and season with salt and pepper. Pour over the chicken and mix well, then thread the chicken on to the soaked skewers.

2 Heat a griddle pan until very hot and lay the skewers on it. Cook for about 10 minutes, turning the skewers occasionally, until the chicken is cooked through. Meanwhile, warm the pitta breads in a low oven, then cut a slit along one side to make them into pockets.

3 To make the dressing, mix the yoghurt and mint together, then season to taste.

4 Fill the pitta breads with lettuce, tomato and sliced onion. Remove the cooked chicken from the skewers and pile into the pitta breads. Drizzle with the dressing and serve.

Menu

*Spicy Chicken
Kebabs*
~
*Classic Healthy
Coleslaw
(p.191)*
~
*Meringues with
Cream & Blueberries
(p.223)*

Stir-fried Chicken
with Chilli & Sweet Basil

Serves 2

1 tablespoon vegetable oil
2 chicken breast fillets, thinly sliced
2 cloves garlic, crushed
2 large red chillies, seeded and sliced
½ onion, cut into 3cm chunks
3 tablespoons Thai fish sauce
1 tablespoon dark soy sauce
1 tablespoon brown sugar
20g sweet fresh basil leaves
Steamed rice, to serve

Menu

Stir-fried Chicken
with Chilli &
Sweet Basil
~
Stir-fried Greens
with Shiitake
Mushrooms (p.179)
~
Lychees with Orange
& Ginger (p.229)

Tip

Before starting any stir-fry recipe, be sure to have all the ingredients prepared – once you have started cooking there will be no time for ingredient preparation.

1 Heat a wok over a high heat until smoking. Add the oil and then the chicken, garlic and chillies. Stir-fry for 1 minute, then add the onion. Continue stir-frying for 5 minutes, or until the chicken is cooked through.

2 Pour in the fish sauce and soy sauce, and sprinkle over the sugar. Bring to the boil and scatter with sweet basil. Serve immediately with steamed rice.

Chicken Satay Skewers
with Sweet Chilli Sauce

Serves 8

2 skinless, boneless chicken breast
   fillets
1 tablespoon crunchy peanut butter
1 tablespoon soy sauce
Pinch of hot chilli powder
80ml hot water
Sweet chilli sauce and cucumber, cut
   into sticks, to serve

1 Soak 16 bamboo skewers in cold water for at least 20 minutes. Cut each chicken breast fillet lengthways into 8 long strips and thread each one on to a soaked skewer. Set aside.

2 Put the peanut butter in a small saucepan with the soy sauce, chilli powder and the hot water. Stir over a gentle heat, allowing the sauce to bubble until it has thickened slightly.

3 Preheat the grill to medium. Brush the satay sauce all over the chicken and place the skewers on a baking tray. Grill for 8–10 minutes, turning occasionally, until the chicken is cooked through. Serve hot or warm with sweet chilli dipping sauce and cucumber sticks.

Menu

*Chicken Satay
Skewers with Sweet
Chilli Sauce*
~
*Rice Vermicelli with
Pork & Vegetables
(p.63)*
~
*Chilled Mandarin &
Lemon Mousse (p.233)*

Southern Fried Chicken

Makes 8

8 chicken thighs or drumsticks
600ml milk
1 tablespoon Tabasco or other hot
   sauce
120g plain flour
1 teaspoon ground black pepper
1 teaspoon cayenne pepper
¼ teaspoon salt
1 egg, beaten
450g white vegetable fat

1 Put the chicken pieces in a large saucepan, preferably in a single layer. Add the milk and hot sauce and leave to marinate for at least 2 hours.

2 Mix the flour, pepper, cayenne pepper and salt together in a bowl.

3 Bring the chicken to the boil, then reduce the heat and simmer for 20 minutes. Drain well, then pat dry and leave to cool for 20 minutes.

4 Dip the chicken pieces first in the seasoned flour, then the egg and then in the flour again.

5 Heat the vegetable fat in a large frying pan until very hot. Add the chicken and cook for 4-5 minutes until golden brown. Drain on kitchen paper.

Menu

*Southern Fried
Chicken*
~
*Chef's Salad
(p.197)*
~
*Berry Ice Lollies
(p.214)*

Spicy Chicken Enchiladas

Serves 4

Two 185ml jars prepared mole poblano
   paste
3 tablespoons peanut butter
250ml chicken stock
Eight 20cm corn tortillas
450g cooked, shredded Grilled Spiced
   Chicken (page 37)
Salt and freshly ground black pepper
1 small onion, finely chopped
300g grated Cheddar cheese
Crème fraîche or soured cream, and
   refried beans, to serve

1 Preheat the barbecue grill to medium
indirect heat.

2 Mix the mole poblano paste and peanut butter
together in a medium saucepan over a low heat.
Mash together until melted. Gradually add enough of
the chicken stock to make a smooth, thick sauce.

3 Warm the corn tortillas by wrapping them
in aluminium foil and putting them on the
barbecue for 3–4 minutes.

4 Spread about a quarter of the mole sauce in
the bottom of a large size aluminium foil tray
(33 x 20cm). Lay one tortilla on a plate and top with about 50g shredded chicken. Season lightly with salt and pepper and sprinkle over a little of the onion, then some of the cheese. Roll up and place, seam-side down, in the aluminium foil tray. Repeat with the remaining tortillas and filling ingredients, reserving about 55g of the cheese.

5 Spoon the remaining mole sauce over the
enchiladas and sprinkle with the reserved
cheese. Cover the tray loosely with aluminium foil
and transfer to the barbecue.

6 Cook for 15 minutes until the enchiladas are
heated through and the sauce is bubbling.

7 Transfer the enchiladas to serving plates and
drizzle each with a little crème fraîche or
soured cream. Serve immediately with a spoonful
of refried beans.

Menu

Spicy Chicken Enchiladas

~

Caesar Salad
(p.194)

~

Grilled Corn Cobs
with Flavoured
Butter (p.174)

Club Sandwiches

Serves 6

18 slices white bread
3 large tomatoes, thinly sliced
3 cooked chicken breasts, thinly sliced
Salt and freshly ground black pepper
6 tablespoons mayonnaise, preferably
  homemade
18 lean back bacon rashers, fried until
  crisp
Crisp lettuce leaves

Menu

Club Sandwiches
~
*Old-fashioned
English Chips (p.164)*
~
*Tomato Salsa
(p.162)*
~
*Caramel Ice Cream
(p.217)*

Tip
Make sure you eat your freshly made club sandwich straight away to prevent your toasted bread from going soggy with the mayonnaise.

1 Lightly toast the bread. Lay 6 pieces on a board and top each one with slices of tomato. Pile the sliced chicken on top and season with salt and freshly ground pepper.

2 Put a second slice of toast over the chicken and spread with the mayonnaise. Lay 3 bacon rashers on top of each one and arrange some lettuce leaves over the bacon.

3 Top with the remaining toast, halve the sandwiches diagonally and secure with cocktail sticks.

Stuffed Cabbage Leaves

Serves 4

8 large leaves of a dark variety of
  cabbage, such as Savoy
1 tablespoon sunflower oil
1 bay leaf
2 large onions, chopped
2 carrots, chopped
3 cloves garlic, crushed
400g can chopped tomatoes
300ml chicken stock
300ml red wine
Salt and freshly ground black pepper
450g chicken, chopped
6 tablespoons fresh breadcrumbs
15g chopped fresh parsley
2 tablespoons chopped fresh sage
1 teaspoon dried oregano

1 Cut out the hard stalk at the base of the cabbage leaves. Bring a large pan of water to the boil. Add the cabbage leaves and bring back to the boil, then cook for 30 seconds, or until the leaves are softened. Pour the leaves into a colander and set aside to drain. Return the pan to the heat and add the oil, bay leaf, onions, carrots and garlic. Stir, then cook gently for 10 minutes, or until the onions have softened slightly. Transfer half the mixture to a bowl, leaving the bay leaf in the pan, and reserve this for the stuffing.

2 Add the tomatoes, stock and wine to the pan. Bring to the boil. Reduce the heat. Cook for 15 minutes, stirring occasionally.

3 Preheat the oven to 180°C/350°F/ Gas mark 4. Add the chicken, breadcrumbs, parsley, sage and oregano to the reserved onion mixture. Season and stir until the ingredients are well combined. Press the mixture with the back of the spoon so that it binds, then divide it into 8 portions.

4 Dry the cabbage leaves on a clean tea towel. Lay each leaf down with the side with protruding veins uppermost. Put some chicken mixture slightly off-centre, nearer to the stalk end of the leaf. Fold the stalk end over the filling, then fold the sides up and roll up into a parcel. Put the leaves in a deep ovenproof dish with the end of the parcel down.

5 Stir the sauce, season if necessary, and ladle it over the cabbage leaves. Cover and cook in the oven for 45 minutes, or until the leaves are tender and the filling is cooked through.

Menu

*Stuffed
Cabbage Leaves*
~
*Broccoli Pilaf
(p.205)*
~
*Chocolate Mousse
(p.232)*

Chicken Hunter-style

Serves 4–6

50g plain flour
Salt and freshly ground black pepper
1.25kg chicken portions
3–4 tablespoons vegetable oil
1 onion, sliced
450g mushrooms, sliced
1 clove garlic, crushed
60ml dry white wine
125ml chicken stock or water
400g can chopped tomatoes
1 tablespoon chopped fresh oregano
1½ teaspoons chopped fresh thyme
Fresh oregano or thyme sprigs, to
   garnish
Freshly cooked spaghetti, to serve

1 Put the flour in a plastic bag and season with salt and pepper; shake to mix. Drop the chicken portions into the bag, one at a time, and shake to coat with the flour. Gently tap off any excess and put the floured chicken on a plate.

2 Heat the oil in a casserole over a medium-high heat. Add the chicken and cook until golden on all sides, turning as necessary. Transfer to a plate.

3 Add the onion and mushrooms to the oil still in the casserole, adding a little more if needed, and cook, stirring frequently, for 7 minutes, or until golden. Add the garlic and cook for a further 20–30 seconds.

4 Pour in the wine and stir to scrape up any cooking residue on the casserole, then add the stock or water and the tomatoes. Season with salt and pepper and replace the chicken with any juices that have seeped from it.

5 Bring to the boil, reduce the heat to low and cover the casserole. Simmer for about 40 minutes, or until the chicken is tender and cooked through and the juices are thickened. Baste the chicken occasionally, if necessary, during cooking.

6 Tilt the casserole to skim off any excess fat, then stir in the chopped herbs. Garnish with oregano or thyme sprigs and serve with freshly cooked spaghetti.

Menu

Chicken Hunter-style
~
*Luxury
Mashed Potatoes
(p.166)*
~
*Hot Vegetable Salad
(p.184)*
~
Pumpkin Pie (p.220)

Halloween Chicken

Serves 4

3 tablespoons light olive oil

350g smoked sausage, cut into 5mm
   slices

900g chicken thighs, cut in half

1 onion, finely chopped

2 sticks celery, finely sliced

2 cloves garlic, crushed

1 green pepper, seeded and finely
   chopped

2 tablespoons plain flour

400g can chopped tomatoes

450ml chicken stock

Salt and freshly ground black pepper

2 tablespoons chopped fresh parsley

1 Heat 2 tablespoons oil in a large casserole. Add the sausage slices and brown for 3-4 minutes. Remove with a slotted spoon and set aside.

2 Add the chicken pieces and brown, a few at a time, for 3-4 minutes. Remove with a slotted spoon and combine with the sausage.

3 Pour the remaining oil into the casserole. Add the onion, celery, garlic and pepper and cook, stirring to prevent them burning, for 10 minutes. Stir in the flour and cook for a further 5 minutes.

4 Add the tomatoes and chicken stock, then bring to the boil. Add the sausage and chicken, stir well and season with salt and pepper. Cover and simmer gently for 40 minutes. Check the seasoning and just before serving stir in the parsley.

Honey-orange Chicken

Serves 4

1.5kg whole chicken
Juice of 2 oranges (about 185ml)
3 cloves garlic, crushed
5 tablespoons clear honey
1 tablespoon chopped chipotles in
   adobo

1 Stand the chicken on a chopping board with its tail end upwards. Using a large, sharp knife or poultry shears, cut down one side of the backbone. Repeat down the other side of the backbone and remove it.

2 Lay the chicken, skin side up, and press down to crack the breastbone and flatten the bird.

3 In a non-metallic dish large enough to hold the bird, mix together the orange juice, garlic, honey and chipotles. Add the chicken, skin side down, and leave to marinate in the refrigerator for about 1 hour.

4 Preheat the barbecue grill to medium direct heat.

5 Wrap 2 average-sized bricks in a double thickness of aluminium foil. Put the chicken, skin side down, on the barbecue grill and top with a baking tray. Put the bricks on top of the baking tray.

6 Grill for 5 minutes, then remove the baking tray and bricks and turn the chicken over. Brush with any remaining marinade. Replace the baking tray and bricks. Keep removing the bricks and turning every 5–10 minutes, brushing with the marinade, for a total cooking time of about 35 minutes, ending skin side down. The chicken should be golden and the skin very crisp. The juices should run clear.

7 Transfer the chicken to a clean chopping board and cut in half through the breastbone. Remove the leg quarters and separate the drumsticks from the thighs. Cut the breasts in half crossways to give 8 pieces. Serve immediately.

Menu

Honey-orange
Chicken
~
Luxury Mashed
Potato (p.166)
~
Braised Fennel
(p.177)

Chicken Kiev

Serves 4

120g butter, softened
1 tablespoon lemon juice
1 clove garlic, mashed with a little salt
1 tablespoon finely chopped fresh
    parsley
4 large part-boned chicken breasts,
    with wings attached, skinned
Salt and freshly ground black pepper
75g plain flour
2 eggs
75g fresh white breadcrumbs
Vegetable oil, for deep-frying
Fresh parsley sprigs, to garnish

Menu

~
Chicken Kiev
~
*Duchesse Potatoes
(p.166)*
~
*Spiced Courgettes
(p.185)*
~
*Mango Ice Cream
(p.216)*

1 Cream the butter, lemon juice, garlic and parsley in a small bowl until well blended. Chill until beginning to firm up, about 20 minutes.

2 Place each chicken breast between cling film and gently roll the meat with a rolling pin to flatten it without making any holes in it. Turn the breasts with the wings down and season.

3 Scrape the butter on to a piece of cling film and roll into a thin sausage shape. Cut into 4 pieces and lay a piece on each chicken breast.

4 Starting at the far end, roll up the chicken fillet around the butter towards the wing joint, tucking in the sides. Make sure the butter is completely enclosed.

5 Put the flour in a plastic bag and put a chicken breast in the bag. Twist the bag to close the end and roll the chicken gently to coat it completely in flour. Repeat with the remaining chicken.

6 Beat the eggs in a shallow bowl and put the breadcrumbs in another bowl. Dip a piece of floured chicken in the egg, turning to coat the entire portion, then into the breadcrumbs, rolling to coat it completely. Repeat with the remaining chicken, egg and breadcrumbs. Arrange on a plate, cover and chill for at least 2 hours or overnight.

7 Heat the oil for deep-frying to 185°C/365°F, or until a small cube of day-old bread browns in about 60 seconds. Add the chicken pieces and deep-fry gently for about 5 minutes, turning once, until crisp and golden. Drain well on kitchen paper and serve immediately, garnished with parsley.

Traditional Roast Chicken

Serves 4

150g sliced white bread, crusts
  removed
50g butter, softened
1 onion, chopped
1 stick celery, finely chopped
1 clove garlic, crushed
115g pork sausage meat, crumbled
Zest of ½ lemon
1 egg, lightly beaten
1 tablespoon chopped fresh sage
½ teaspoon paprika
Salt and freshly ground black pepper
1.5kg whole chicken
Whole fresh sage leaves and thyme
  sprigs

For the gravy
2 teaspoons plain flour
125ml red or white wine
300ml chicken stock

1 Preheat the oven to 220°C/425°F/Gas mark 7.
Cut the bread into 1cm cubes and put into a
large bowl. Set aside.

2 Melt 25g of the butter in a frying pan over a
medium heat until foaming. Add the onion and
celery and cook for 5-7 minutes until softened and translucent. Add the garlic and cook for a further minute. Add the sausage meat. Increase the heat and cook for a further 5 minutes, stirring once or twice only, until the sausage meat is browned and cooked through. Remove any excess fat that may have come from the sausage meat with a metal spoon and discard.

3 Add the sausage meat mixture, lemon zest, egg, sage and paprika to the bread. Season well with salt and pepper and mix together thoroughly.

4 Wash the chicken inside and out and dry with kitchen paper. Turn the bird so that the wings are nearest you with the breast uppermost. Take a handful of the stuffing mixture and put it under the flap of skin between the wings - you'll probably fit two handfuls. Press in well, then pull the skin down to cover the stuffing. Using poultry skewers or

continued ...

Menu

*Traditional
Roast Chicken*
~
*Brussels Sprouts
with Sweet Potatoes
(p.183)*
~
*Carrots with Maple
Syrup (p.182)*

cocktail sticks, secure the skin underneath the bird. Take the remaining stuffing and stuff the body cavity.

5 Smear the breast and legs of the chicken with the remaining butter. Season well and sprinkle with sage leaves and thyme.

6 Put the chicken into a roasting tin and cook for about 1 hour 20 minutes, or allowing 20 minutes per 450g plus 20 minutes, reducing the oven temperature to 190°C/375°F/Gas mark 5 after the first 20 minutes. Every 20 minutes or so, carefully baste the bird with the juices in the tin.

7 To check if the bird is cooked, remove it from the oven. Using a skewer or small sharp knife, pierce the bird in the thickest part of the thigh. If the juices run clear, without a trace of pink, the bird is cooked. Gently pull the leg away from the body. If it gives easily, the bird is cooked. Transfer the bird to a carving board and leave to rest for at least 10 minutes. Remove the stuffing from the body cavity and transfer to a serving dish. Sprinkle with more sage leaves and thyme sprigs, if desired. Keep warm. Carve the bird and serve with gravy.

8 To make the gravy, after transferring the bird to a carving board, remove as much fat as possible from the roasting tin. Tilt the tin so that all the juices collect in one corner and, using a large metal spoon, skim the fat off the top and discard. Put the tin over a medium heat. Add the plain flour and

whisk well until smooth. Gradually add the red or white wine. Bring to the boil and simmer gently for 2–3 minutes until thickened. Gradually add the chicken stock, or a combination of chicken stock and the cooking water from the vegetables or potatoes. Whisk until smooth. Bring to the boil and simmer for 5–7 minutes until thickened and reduced. Taste for seasoning. Simmer for a few more minutes to reduce if the flavour is weak. Taste again and add seasoning as necessary.

Stuffing Variation

Add 1 peeled, chopped apple and 25g of chopped walnuts to the bread along with the sausage meat mixture. Cook 225g of mixed long-grain and wild rice according to the packet instructions until tender. Add 4 chopped spring onions, 1 shredded carrot, 125g of sliced mushrooms, 1 crushed clove garlic, 2 tablespoons of soy sauce, 1 tablespoon of honey, 1 tablespoon of vegetable oil and mix well. Use to stuff the bird and cook as above.

Grilled Spiced Chicken

Serves 4

2 tablespoons fennel seeds
1 tablespoon coriander seeds
1 tablespoon black peppercorns
1½ teaspoons chilli flakes
2 teaspoons cayenne pepper
2 tablespoons salt
1 teaspoon ground cinnamon
1.5kg whole chicken

1 Preheat the barbecue grill to medium indirect heat. Heat a small, dry frying pan on the hob over a medium heat and add the fennel seeds, coriander seeds and black peppercorns. Cook for 1-2 minutes, shaking the pan frequently, until the spices smell aromatic and begin to brown. If you have an extractor fan, switch it on full; if not, open the window and add the chilli flakes to the pan. Stand back to avoid the fumes and shake the pan for about 30 seconds. Remove the pan from the heat and quickly transfer the mixture to a plate to cool.

2 When the mixture is cool, transfer to a mortar and pestle or spice grinder and grind to a fine powder. Stir in the cayenne pepper, salt and cinnamon.

3 Wash the chicken inside and out and dry thoroughly with kitchen paper. Sprinkle about 2 tablespoons of the spice mixture inside the chicken and all over the skin, rubbing it in well. If you have time, set aside to marinate for at least 30 minutes.

4 Cook the chicken over indirect medium heat for 1 hour 20 minutes, or until golden and the juices run clear. The legs should pull away from the body easily – if they don't, cook the chicken for a further 10 minutes then try again.

5 Remove the chicken from the barbecue and leave to rest for 10 minutes before carving. Otherwise, leave until cold and carve or tear the meat from the bones to use in another recipe.

Menu

Grilled Spiced Chicken

~

Latkes (p.171)

~

Cauliflower & Leek Patties (p.188)

~

Summer Berry Shortcakes (p.246)

Chicken & Vegetable Pie

Serves 4–6

1.3kg whole chicken
1 large carrot, cut into chunks
1 onion, halved
1 stick celery, cut into chunks
1 bay leaf
1 fresh thyme sprig
6 black peppercorns
Salt and freshly ground black pepper
450g mixed spring vegetables (haricots verts, baby carrots, asparagus, peas, baby leeks, courgettes, baby fennel)
50g butter
2 teaspoons fresh thyme leaves
40g plain flour, plus extra for dusting
125ml double cream
675g ready-made puff pastry
1 egg, beaten

1 Put the chicken, carrot, onion, celery, bay leaf, thyme sprig, peppercorns and enough water to cover in a large pan, cover and gently simmer for 1 hour, skimming off any scum from the surface. Remove the pan from the heat and leave the chicken and stock to cool. Remove the chicken and set aside. Strain the stock into a clean pan and bring back to the boil. Simmer until reduced to 900ml. Season. Skin the chicken and cut the flesh into chunks.

2 Slice the spring vegetables. Place in the boiling stock and bring back to the boil. Blanch for 3 minutes. Remove with a slotted spoon and set aside, reserving the stock. Melt the butter in a pan, add the thyme leaves and flour and stir well. Gradually add the reserved stock, stirring well, until smooth. Increase the heat, bring to the boil, stirring continuously, and simmer for 2 minutes. Remove from the heat and stir in the cream, reserved chicken and vegetables. Season.

3 Preheat the oven to 200°C/400°F/Gas mark 6. Roll out the prepared pastry on a lightly floured surface and cut a strip just larger than the rim of the pie dish. Brush the rim of the dish with water and attach the strip. Cut another piece to make the lid. Spoon the filling into the pie dish. Dampen the pastry strip and top with the pastry lid. Cut a small slit in the centre of the lid. Crimp the edges to make a decorative edge. Use pastry trimmings to decorate the pie, then brush with beaten egg. Transfer to the centre of the oven and bake for 25 minutes, or until the pastry is golden and the filling is bubbling.

Menu

Chicken & Vegetable Pie
~
Spiced Baked Apples (p.224)

Spicy Peanut Chicken
Noodles

Serves 4

115g flat rice noodles
Salt
2 tablespoons crunchy peanut butter
Pinch of hot chilli powder
1 tablespoon dark soy sauce
180ml coconut cream
120ml hot water
2 ready-cooked chicken breast fillets,
    shredded
4 spring onions, sliced
Small bunch of fresh coriander,
    roughly chopped
Green salad, to serve

Menu

Spicy
Peanut Chicken
Noodles
~
Apple Cake
Bars
(p.241)

1 Cook the noodles in a saucepan of boiling salted water for 4 minutes, or until tender, then drain well.

2 Meanwhile, put the peanut butter in a small saucepan with the chilli powder, soy sauce, coconut cream and hot water.

3 Stir over a gentle heat until combined, then add the chicken and spring onions. Warm through for a few minutes, and then stir in the noodles and coriander. Serve immediately with a green salad.

Tip

Although this recipe calls for chicken breast fillets, if you happen to have any leftover cold roast chicken or pork in the refrigerator, these will work just as well.

Chicken Tikka

Serves 6

6 chicken breast fillets, each cut into
   8 pieces
1 yellow onion, coarsely chopped
3 cloves garlic, coarsely chopped
2.5cm fresh root ginger, peeled
240ml natural yoghurt
2 tablespoons toasted sesame oil
Juice of ½ lemon
3 teaspoons ground coriander
1 teaspoon ground turmeric
1 teaspoon chilli flakes
1 teaspoon salt
1 onion, cut into quarters and
   separated into layers
Steamed spinach, to serve

Menu

Chicken Tikka
~
Coconut Rice
(p.206)

1 Put the chicken in a large non-metallic bowl and set aside.

2 Put the chopped onion, garlic and ginger in a food processor and process to make a smooth paste. Add the yoghurt, sesame oil, lemon juice, coriander, turmeric, chilli and salt, and process until smooth.

3 Pour the marinade over the chicken, toss to coat, then leave to marinate in the refrigerator overnight. Stir to redistribute the marinade. Soak 12 bamboo skewers in water overnight.

4 Assemble the tikka kebabs. Thread four pieces of chicken on to each skewer, alternating each piece with an onion layer. Baste the kebabs with more marinade, cover and return to the refrigerator until ready to cook.

5 To cook, prepare a barbecue, or preheat the grill. Cook for several minutes on each side, turning once. Serve with steamed spinach.

Lemon Chicken
with Herb Tagliatelle

Serves 2

2 large boned chicken breasts, skin on
2 tablespoons plain flour, well
  seasoned
50g butter
1 tablespoon olive oil
Salt and freshly ground black pepper
200g fresh tagliatelle
30g chopped fresh herbs
2 teaspoons grated lemon zest
2 tablespoons fresh lemon juice
1 tablespoon drained capers, roughly
  chopped if large

1 Wash and dry the chicken breasts. Put the
  seasoned flour on to a plate and coat both sides
of each chicken breast. Shake to remove any excess
flour. Set aside.

2 Melt half the butter with the oil in a frying pan
  until foaming. Add the chicken breasts, skin side
down, and cook for about 10 minutes over a low
heat until deep golden.

3 Turn the chicken
  breasts and cook
on the second side for
a further 10 minutes.

4 Turn the chicken breasts again and cook for a
  further 5-10 minutes, or until the chicken is
cooked through.

5 Meanwhile, bring a large saucepan of salted
  water to the boil. Add the pasta and cook for
2-3 minutes, or until al dente. Drain well, then
sprinkle in the chopped fresh herbs and stir.

6 Remove the cooked chicken breasts from the
  pan. Add the remaining butter and cook until
foaming and beginning to brown. Add the lemon zest
and juice and the capers. Scrape up any bits from the
bottom of the pan. Remove from the heat and season.

7 Slice the chicken breasts thickly on the
  diagonal. Divide the pasta among serving dishes
and top with the sliced chicken. Drizzle with the
lemon butter sauce and serve immediately.

Menu

Lemon
Chicken with Herb
Tagliatelle
~
Courgette Bread
(p.208)
~
Peanut Butter
Brownies
(p.240)

Spicy Chicken Sausages

Serves 4

25g butter
1 onion, finely chopped
2 cloves garlic, finely chopped
1 tablespoon paprika
675g boned chicken thighs
2 red chillies, seeded
Small bunch of fresh parsley
10 thyme sprigs
50g fresh white breadcrumbs
1 egg, beaten
Salt and freshly ground black pepper
4 tablespoons sunflower oil

1 Melt the butter in a frying pan. Add the onion and garlic and fry for 5 minutes. Add the paprika and fry for 1 minute. Take off the heat and leave to cool.

2 Put the boneless chicken thighs in a food processor and process for a few seconds until the meat is finely chopped. Don't over-process or it will become a paste. Transfer to a mixing bowl.

3 Finely chop the chilli, parsley and thyme with a mezzaluna, and mix into the chopped chicken with the cooled onion mixture and breadcrumbs. Add the beaten egg and stir well. Season well with salt and pepper.

4 Divide the mixture into 12 balls and roll the sausages. Heat the oil in a frying pan and fry the sausages, turning regularly, for 15–20 minutes, or until browned and cooked through.

Menu

Spicy Chicken Sausages

~

Beetroot & Onion Mash (p.182)

~

New England Blueberry Pancakes (p.226)

Apple & Ginger Turkey Sandwiches

Serves 4

4 turkey breast steaks
1 large onion, thickly sliced
1 tablespoon olive oil
2 dessert apples, such as Granny Smith, cored and thickly sliced crossways
Ciabatta bread
Salt and freshly ground pepper
Mayonnaise
Rocket leaves, to serve

For the apple marinade

125ml apple juice, preferably cloudy
2 tablespoons cider vinegar
2 teaspoons finely grated fresh ginger
1 clove garlic, crushed
3 cloves

1 For the marinade, mix the apple juice, cider vinegar, ginger, garlic and cloves together in a small saucepan over a low heat. Bring to the boil and simmer for 2 minutes, then remove from the heat. Leave to cool.

Menu

Apple & Ginger Turkey Sandwiches
~
Classic Healthy Coleslaw (p.191)

2 Put the turkey steaks in a single layer in a non-metallic dish. Pour the cooled marinade over, then cover and marinate for at least 1 hour.

3 Preheat the barbecue grill to high direct heat. Brush the onion slices with the olive oil and cook over high direct heat for 10-12 minutes, turning often and carefully, until golden and tender.

4 Cook the apple slices with the onions for 4-5 minutes, turning often until golden and tender.

5 Lift the turkey steaks from the marinade, shaking off the excess. Cook, alongside the onion and apple slices, over high direct heat for 6-8 minutes, turning once halfway through the cooking time.

6 Top the ciabatta bread with a turkey steak, some onion, 2 apple slices and some mayonnaise. Serve with a few rocket leaves.

Roast Turkey with

Sausage & Sage Stuffing

Serves 10–12

4.5–5.5kg turkey with giblets, neck and
  wing tips removed for gravy
225g butter, softened
½ teaspoon dried thyme
½ teaspoon dried sage
500ml chicken or turkey stock
Watercress or herb sprigs, to garnish

For the stuffing
25g butter
1 onion, chopped
2–3 sticks celery, thinly sliced
450g sausage meat
2 cloves garlic, crushed
2 tablespoons chopped sage
1 tablespoon dried thyme
120g pecan nuts, toasted and chopped
  (optional)
450g firm-textured white bread, crusts
  removed, cut into small cubes
500–750ml chicken or turkey stock,
  preferably homemade
Salt and freshly ground black pepper
2 eggs, lightly beaten

1 To prepare the stuffing, melt the butter in a large saucepan. Add the onion and celery and cook, stirring frequently, for about 4 minutes, until the vegetables begin to soften. Add the sausage meat and garlic and cook, stirring, for 4 minutes, until the meat is no longer pink. Stir in the sage, thyme and pecan nuts, if using, and remove from the heat.

2 Add the bread to the stuffing and combine it with the other ingredients. Stir in half the stock and season with salt and pepper. Add more stock if the mixture seems dry, then leave to cool slightly.

3 Stir the beaten eggs into the stuffing. Add more stock, if necessary, so that the stuffing holds together but is not too wet. Set aside. (This can be prepared a day ahead, covered and chilled.)

4 To prepare the turkey, preheat the oven to 160°C/325°F/Gas mark 3. Rinse the turkey

Menu

*Roast Turkey
with Sausage & Sage
Stuffing*
~
*Sweet Potato Casserole
with Marshmallow
Topping (p.176)*
~
*Braised Sugar Snaps
with Lettuce (p.178)*
~
*Double-crust Apple Pie
(p.228)*

cavity and dry with kitchen paper, then season. Cream the butter, thyme, sage and salt and pepper together in a bowl. Starting with the neck end, separate the skin from the meat on both sides of the breast. Spread half the butter under the skin, pushing it far under the skin. Rub the remaining butter over the turkey. Tuck the neck skin under the bird and close with a skewer.

5 Spoon the stuffing into the cavity and secure the opening with skewers. Tie the legs together with string. Alternatively, stuff the neck end before tucking the skin under and securing it. Put any leftover stuffing in a greased baking dish and cover with foil: this can be baked in the oven with the turkey for about 1 hour at the end of cooking.

6 Set the turkey on a rack in a roasting tin and pour about 250ml of the stock into the tin. Roast the turkey for 3½–4½ hours, or until a meat

thermometer inserted into the thickest part of the thigh reads 82°C/180°F. Baste the turkey frequently, adding a little more stock or water as necessary. Check the cooking after 3 hours by piercing a thigh with a skewer - the juices should run clear, if not, continue cooking. Cover the turkey with foil if it browns too quickly. Transfer it to a plate and leave, covered with a tent of foil, for at least 30 minutes.

7 Pour the cooking juices into a bowl and leave to stand 5 minutes, then skim off as much fat as possible.

8 To serve, remove the skewers and spoon the stuffing into a serving bowl; keep warm. Carve the turkey on to a large heated platter or directly on to serving plates and serve with stuffing, gravy and all the trimmings, and garnished with watercress sprigs.

Tip
Frozen turkeys are best thawed in the refrigerator. The key to this method is to plan ahead and allow 24 hours for every 4-5 pounds of turkey weight.

Spicy Turkey Meatballs

Serves 4

450g boneless turkey breast
225g pancetta or bacon, chopped
2 cloves garlic, chopped
1 teaspoon salt
Pinch of ground cinnamon
Pinch of ground allspice
Large pinch of chilli flakes
Salt and freshly ground black pepper
25g fresh breadcrumbs
1 egg, lightly beaten
4 tablespoons olive oil
1 onion, finely chopped
1kg ripe tomatoes, skinned and
   roughly chopped
150ml red wine
1 teaspoon dried oregano
2 tablespoons chopped fresh basil,
   plus extra to garnish
Pinch of sugar
350g fresh taglioni or tagliatelle
Freshly grated Parmesan cheese,
   to serve

1 Cut the turkey into chunks and put into a food processor. Add the pancetta or bacon, garlic, salt, cinnamon, allspice, chilli flakes and pepper. Process until finely chopped. Transfer to a bowl, add the breadcrumbs and egg and mix. Shape the mixture into balls. Chill at least 30 minutes.

2 Heat 2 tablespoons of the oil, add the onion and fry for 5 minutes. Add tomatoes, red wine, oregano, half the basil and the sugar and bring to the boil. Cover and simmer for 30 minutes.

3 Heat the remaining oil in a frying pan over a medium heat. Add the meatballs in batches and cook for 5 minutes, turning frequently, until golden. As they brown, add them to the tomato sauce. Bring the sauce back to the boil and simmer for 20–30 minutes until the meatballs are cooked and the sauce is thickened. Stir in the remaining basil.

4 Meanwhile, bring a large saucepan of salted water to a rolling boil. Add the pasta and cook for 2–3 minutes until al dente. Drain well.

5 Divide the pasta among serving dishes and top with the meatball sauce. Garnish with extra basil and serve with Parmesan cheese.

Menu

Spicy Turkey Meatballs
~
Panzanella (p.198)
~
Chocolate-covered Doughnuts (p.238)

Turkey-stuffed Peppers

Serves 4

Grated zest and juice of 1 lime

4 spring onions, chopped

2 cloves garlic, crushed

1 carrot, coarsely grated

8 closed-cap mushrooms, thinly sliced

Salt and freshly ground black pepper

2 tablespoons extra virgin olive oil, plus extra for oiling and brushing

450g boneless turkey breast fillets, cut into fine strips

4 large green peppers, halved and seeded with stalks in place

30g chopped fresh coriander

Tip

You can vary the ingredients used to stuff these peppers. Try using chicken, pork, or lean steak. For a vegetarian version just add rice to fill it out.

1 Mix the lime zest and juice in a bowl. Add the spring onions, garlic, carrot, mushrooms and plenty of seasoning. Stir in the oil, then mix in the turkey. Cover and chill for at least 1 hour. If you can, make this in advance and chill for several hours.

2 Preheat the oven to 200°C/400°F/Gas mark 6. Oil a large, shallow ovenproof dish, then place the pepper halves in it, supporting them against each other so they sit neatly. Brush with a little oil and bake for 20 minutes.

3 Stir the turkey mixture well, then divide it among the pepper 'boats'. Drizzle with a little extra oil to moisten the filling. Bake for a further 20–30 minutes, or until both peppers and filling are well cooked and browned on top.

4 Sprinkle the chopped coriander over the peppers and filling, and serve at once.

Menu

Turkey-stuffed Peppers
~
Chickpea & Tomato Salad
(p.195)
~
Cherry Clafoutis
(p.243)

MEAT

- Tortilla Wraps with Honey Roast Ham & Pepper Slaw
- Grilled Cheese & Tomato Sandwiches with Bacon
- Italian Submarine Sandwiches
- New Potato & Crispy Bacon Salad
- Tomato Pasta with Italian Sausage & Lentils
- Quick Mushroom Carbonara
- Chop Suey
- Cowboy Beans & Sausages
- Rice Vermicelli with Pork & Vegetables
- Spanish Pork with Tomatoes & Chorizo
- Baked Country Ham
- Kansas City Pork Ribs
- Bacon Cheeseburgers
- Beef & Onion Pies
- Pasta Shells Filled with Bolognese
- Beef Stew with Herb Dumplings
- Easy Burritos
- Roast Rib of Beef with Caramelized Shallots
- Old-fashioned Meatloaf
- Beef Stew with Star Anise
- Braised Lamb Shanks with Mirepoix Vegetables
- Tagine with Prunes & Almonds
- Lamb Meatballs with Buttermilk & Herb Dip
- Papaya Lamb Kebabs
- Kofta
- Roast Leg of Lamb
- Baked Lasagne

CHAPTER TWO

MEAT

Tortilla Wraps with

Honey Roast Ham & Pepper Slaw

Serves 4

8 soft flour tortilla wraps
8 large slices honey roast ham
Few salad leaves

For the pepper slaw
450g white cabbage, finely shredded
225g carrots, grated
2 red peppers, seeded and thinly sliced
225g mayonnaise
175g soured cream or natural yoghurt
1 teaspoon white wine vinegar
Salt and freshly ground black pepper

Menu

*Tortilla Wraps with
Honey Roast Ham &
Pepper Slaw*
~
*Warm Cheese &
Smoked Chilli Dip with
Tortilla Chips (p.163)*
~
*Summer Berry
Shortcakes (p.246)*

1 For the pepper slaw, mix the cabbage, carrots and peppers together in a large bowl. Mix the mayonnaise with the soured cream and vinegar, and season with salt and pepper.

2 Take 8 flour wraps and place a slice of ham in the top centre of each one. Spoon 2-3 tablespoons of the slaw on top with a few salad leaves. Bring up the bottom of the wrap and fold in the sides.

3 Secure each wrap with a cocktail stick and wrap in a napkin.

Grilled Cheese & Tomato

Sandwiches with Bacon

Serves 4

8 slices country-style white bread
55g butter, softened
2 tablespoons Dijon mustard
115–175g Swiss cheese, such as
    Emmental, thinly sliced
115–175g Cheddar cheese,
    thinly sliced
8 thick tomato slices
8 rindless lean back bacon rashers,
    cooked until crisp
Potato crisps, to serve

1 Lay the slices of bread on a board and spread them evenly with butter. Turn the slices over, so the buttered sides are down, and spread the other sides with the mustard.

2 Layer the cheeses, tomato slices and bacon on 4 bread slices, overlapping or trimming the ingredients to fit. Top with the remaining bread, mustard sides down, and press gently to compress the sandwiches.

Menu

Grilled Cheese &
Tomato Sandwiches
with Bacon
~
Caesar Salad (p.194)
~
Apple Sauce Sundae
(p.236)

3 Heat a large, non-stick frying pan over a medium heat.

4 Working in batches, place the sandwiches in the pan and cook for about 3 minutes, pressing down gently and frequently until crisp and golden. Carefully turn and continue cooking for a further 2 minutes, pressing the sandwiches down until they are golden and the cheese is melting and beginning to ooze out. Repeat with the remaining sandwiches.

5 Transfer the sandwiches to a chopping board and slice in half. Serve immediately with crisps.

Italian Submarine

Sandwiches

Serves 4

115g mayonnaise
60g soured cream
1 tablespoon Dijon mustard
4 individual French rolls, about 20cm long
Butter or margarine, softened, for spreading
Crisp lettuce leaves
175g boiled or baked ham, sliced
175g salami
175g cooked chicken or turkey, sliced
120g Emmental cheese, sliced
120g Cheddar cheese, sliced
2 tomatoes, thinly sliced
1 large green pepper, seeded and cut into rings
1 onion, thinly sliced

Menu

Italian Submarine Sandwiches

~

Chef's Salad (p.197)

1 Combine the mayonnaise, soured cream and mustard in a small bowl until well blended.

2 Using a serrated knife, split the rolls horizontally in half. Remove some of the soft bread and spread both halves lightly with butter or margarine. Spread the top halves generously with the mayonnaise mixture.

3 Arrange 2-3 lettuce leaves on the bottom half of each roll, folding them to fit. Layer the remaining ingredients in order on top of the lettuce. Cover with the tops and cut across in half.

New Potato &
Crispy Bacon Salad

Serves 4

1kg small new potatoes, scrubbed
Salt and freshly ground black pepper
275g asparagus spears, woody stalks
  removed
6 cloves garlic, unpeeled
6 tablespoons vegetable oil
200g streaky bacon rashers
225g blue cheese, crumbled
2 tablespoons chopped fresh parsley
1 tablespoon chopped fresh chives

1 Preheat the oven to 200°C/400°F/Gas mark 6.
Put the new potatoes in a saucepan of salted
water. Bring to the boil and cook for 5 minutes.
Drain and put in a roasting tin with the asparagus
and garlic. Season with salt and pepper and drizzle
with oil. Roast in the oven for 45 minutes.

2 Meanwhile, lay the bacon in another roasting
tin and cook in the oven for 10-15 minutes
until brown and crispy. Remove and leave to cool.
Crumble the bacon into small pieces.

3 Once the potatoes are cooked, discard the
garlic. Put the potatoes in a serving dish with
the asparagus, set aside until just warm, then scatter
with the bacon, blue cheese and herbs. Serve warm
or cold.

Menu

*New Potato & Crispy
Bacon Salad*
~
*Emmental & Roasted
Corn Spoon Bread
(p.207)*
~
*Boston Cream Pie
(p.244)*

Tomato Pasta with
Italian Sausage & Lentils

Serves 4

225g Puy or Umbrian lentils
3 tablespoons olive oil
1 onion, finely chopped
500g spicy Italian sausage
2 cloves garlic, crushed
400g can chopped tomatoes
300ml chicken or vegetable stock
Salt and freshly ground black pepper
350g fresh tomato-flavoured tagliatelle
1 tablespoon chopped fresh parsley

1 Pick over the lentils, looking for any grit. Rinse under cold running water and drain well.

2 Heat the oil in a large, deep saucepan and add the onion. Cook for 5-7 minutes over a low heat until soft and starting to brown. Add the sausages and garlic and cook for 3-4 minutes until the sausages start to brown. Add the drained lentils and continue cooking for a further 1 minute.

3 Add the tomatoes and stock. Season lightly with salt and pepper and bring to the boil. Cover, reduce the heat and simmer gently for 40-45 minutes until the sausages and lentils are tender. Check the seasoning.

4 Meanwhile, bring a large saucepan of salted water to a rolling boil. Add the pasta and cook for 2-3 minutes until al dente. Drain well.

5 Divide the pasta among serving dishes and spoon over the sausages and lentils. Sprinkle with the chopped parsley and serve.

Menu

Tomato Pasta
with Italian Sausage
& Lentils
~
Green Bean &
Mozzarella Salad
(p.201)
~
Spiced Baked Apples
(p.224)

Quick Mushroom

Carbonara

Serves 4

Menu

Quick Mushroom Carbonara

~

Hot Vegetable Salad (p.184)

~

Chocolate Fondue with Marshmallows (p.230)

350g dried spaghetti
Salt and freshly ground black pepper
160ml double cream
1 clove garlic
150g pancetta cubes
8 chestnut mushrooms, sliced
4 egg yolks, beaten
25g freshly grated Parmesan cheese

1 Cook the spaghetti in a saucepan of salted boiling water according to the instructions on the packet until al dente. Drain well. Meanwhile, put the cream and garlic clove in a saucepan and bring to the boil. Set aside.

2 Heat a frying pan. Add the pancetta and mushrooms and fry for 4-5 minutes, or until browned. Toss with the spaghetti.

3 Remove the garlic from the cream and pour over the spaghetti. Quickly stir in the egg yolks and Parmesan cheese. Season to taste with salt and pepper and serve immediately.

Chop Suey

Serves 4

2 tablespoons cornflour

3 tablespoons soy sauce

1 tablespoon dry sherry

Salt and freshly ground black pepper

2.5cm piece fresh root ginger, grated
or finely chopped

125ml water

2 tablespoons vegetable oil

450g pork tenderloin or skinless,
boneless chicken breast, cut into thin
strips

1 small head Chinese cabbage, finely
shredded

2–3 sticks celery, thinly sliced on the
diagonal into 11cm pieces

6–8 spring onions, sliced on the
diagonal into 1cm pieces

450g bean sprouts, rinsed

175–240g can water chestnuts, drained
and sliced

150–175g can bamboo shoots, drained
and sliced

2 tablespoons chopped fresh coriander
leaves or parsley

Cooked rice, to serve

Menu

Chop Suey
~
Tropical
Fruit Salad
(p.221)

1 Combine the cornflour, soy sauce, sherry, salt and pepper, ginger and water in a small bowl until well blended; set aside.

2 Heat the oil over a medium-high heat in a wok or large heavy-based frying pan. Add the pork or chicken and stir-fry for about 4 minutes. Stir the cornflour mixture and stir it into the pork – the mixture will thicken as it comes to the boil.

3 Add the cabbage, celery, spring onions, bean sprouts, water chestnuts, bamboo shoots and coriander to the wok and stir-fry for a further 5 minutes, or until the meat is cooked and vegetables are just tender. Serve on a bed of rice.

Cowboy Beans
& Sausages

Serves 4

Menu

Cowboy Beans &
Sausages
~
Maple-baked Acorn
Squash (p.189)
~
Applesauce Sundae
(p.236)

450g dried haricot beans
3 tablespoons oil
2 onions, roughly chopped
2 cloves garlic, crushed
400g can chopped tomatoes
275g smoked bacon, roughly chopped
1 tablespoon black treacle
1 tablespoon mustard powder
2 tablespoons soft brown sugar
16 sausages
Salt and freshly ground black pepper

1 Soak the beans overnight in plenty of cold water. Drain and put in a large saucepan. Cover with water, bring to the boil and boil for 15 minutes. Reduce the heat and simmer for 1 hour.

2 Meanwhile, heat the oil in a large casserole. Add the onions and garlic and cook for 15 minutes. Add the tomatoes, bacon, treacle, mustard powder and sugar and stir well. Preheat the oven to 150°C/ 300°F/Gas mark 2.

3 Add the beans, cover and cook in the oven for 2 hours. Uncover and cook for a further 1 hour.

4 Preheat the grill. Grill the sausages for 15 minutes, turning to ensure even cooking, then cut into bite-sized pieces. Stir the bacon into the beans and cook for a further 20 minutes. Taste and season with salt and pepper before serving.

Rice Vermicelli
with Pork & Vegetables

Serves 4

350g rice vermicelli
350g mixed vegetables (such as broccoli, mangetout and asparagus)
1 tablespoon arrowroot or cornflour
1 teaspoon honey
120ml chicken or vegetable stock
4 tablespoons vegetable oil
4 tablespoons light soy sauce
2 cloves garlic, finely chopped
2.5cm fresh galangal or root ginger, peeled and finely chopped
225g lean pork, sliced into thin 2.5cm squares
1 tablespoon nuoc mam (Vietnamese fish sauce)
1 tablespoon black bean sauce
1 tablespoon chopped fresh basil leaves or coriander, to garnish

1 Cook the noodles according to the instructions on the packet. Rinse under cold running water and set aside.

Menu

Rice Vermicelli with Pork & Vegetables

~

Chicken Satay Skewers with Sweet Chilli Sauce (p.22)

~

Chilled Mandarin & Lemon Mousse (p.233)

2 Prepare the vegetables: cut the broccoli into florets; cut the mangetout in half; cut the asparagus into 5cm pieces. Steam the broccoli and asparagus for 5 minutes until tender but still crisp. Refresh under cold running water and set aside.

3 Blend the arrowroot or cornflour and honey with the stock. Set aside. Heat half the oil in a wok and add the noodles and 1 tablespoon soy sauce. Stir-fry for 30 seconds, then transfer to a serving platter.

4 Add the remaining oil to the wok. Stir-fry the garlic and galangal until they start to change colour. Add the pork and mangetout, and stir-fry until the pork starts to brown. Add the remaining soy sauce, the nuoc mam, black bean sauce, vegetables and stock mixture. Stir until the sauce thickens, then pour over the noodles and garnish with basil or coriander.

Spanish Pork
with Tomatoes & Chorizo

Serves 6

1.25kg belly of pork, in one piece
2 tablespoons sunflower oil
2 onions, finely chopped
4 cloves garlic, finely chopped
200g chorizo sausage, skin removed
  and roughly chopped
1 tablespoon pimentón or paprika
800g can chopped tomatoes
120ml white wine
2 bay leaves
Small bunch of fresh parsley, finely
  chopped
Green salad, to serve

Menu

Spanish Pork
with Tomatoes &
Chorizo
~
Patatas Bravas
(p.167)

Tip
When roasting pork,
score the rind deeply with a
very sharp knife and rub with
oil and salt before cooking to
get a crisp 'crackling'.

1 Preheat the oven to 150°C/300°F/Gas mark 2. Cut the pork into 1cm pieces with a large chopping knife.

2 Heat the oil in a large casserole and brown the meat in batches. Transfer to a bowl. Add the onions and garlic to the casserole and fry for about 10 minutes, or until browned. Add the chorizo to the casserole and fry 5 minutes. Stir in the pimentón.

3 Return the meat to the casserole and add the tomatoes, wine and bay leaves. Cover and cook in the oven for 3 hours.

4 Sprinkle over the parsley before serving, and serve with a green salad.

Baked Country Ham

Serves 20–25

4.9–6kg partially cooked whole ham,
preferably boneless
Whole cloves, for studding
Fresh parsley sprigs, to garnish
Boiled or mashed potato or salad, to serve

For the honey-mustard glaze
2 tablespoons soy sauce
60ml water, plus 2–3 tablespoons
250ml clear honey
125ml Dijon mustard
½–1 teaspoon cornflour

1 Preheat the oven to 160°C/325°F/Gas mark 3.
Put the ham on a rack in a large roasting tin
and add enough water to cover the bottom of the
tin. Insert a meat thermometer in the thickest
part of the ham and roast, uncovered, allowing
20-25 minutes per 450g or until the thermometer
reaches 70°C/160°F. Add more water if needed
during cooking to prevent the ham from drying out.

2 About 1 hour before the ham is ready, combine
the soy sauce, 60ml water, honey and mustard
for the glaze in a small pan. Bring to the boil over
a medium heat, stirring, and then remove from
the heat.

3 Remove the ham
from the oven
and cut off the rind,
leaving a 5mm layer
of white fat. Slash the
surface of the fat
diagonally to create a
diamond pattern and
press a clove in the
middle of each
diamond. Brush with
the glaze and roast for a further 45 minutes, brushing
with more glaze occasionally. Keep the bottom of
the roasting tin covered with water. Transfer the
ham to a serving platter and tent it with foil but do
not let the foil stick to the glazed surface. Set aside.

4 Tilt the roasting tin and skim off any fat from
the tin, then add the remaining glaze to the tin
and set it over a medium heat. Stir 2-3 tablespoons
water into the cornflour until smooth, then stir it
into the glaze and bring to the boil, stirring, until
lightly thickened. Add more blended cornflour or
water, as necessary, and add any juices from the
baked ham. Strain into a gravy boat.

5 Garnish the ham with parsley and serve hot
with the glaze as a sauce.

> **Menu**
>
> Baked Country Ham
> ~
> Luxury Mashed
> Potatoes (p.166)
> ~
> Braised Fennel
> (p.177)
> ~
> Cherry Clafoutis
> (p.243)

Kansas City Pork Ribs

Serves 4

80g dark brown sugar
½ onion, finely chopped
1½ teaspoons celery seeds
1½ teaspoons garlic powder
1½ teaspoons chilli seasoning
1 teaspoon finely ground black pepper
1 teaspoon ground cumin
½ teaspoon cayenne pepper
500ml tomato ketchup
60ml white vinegar or more to taste
2 tablespoons prepared yellow
  mustard
Juice of 1 lime
1 teaspoon liquid smoke (optional)
Salt and freshly ground black pepper
4 tablespoons butter, cubed and chilled
2.7kg baby back pork spare ribs

Menu

*Kansas City
Pork Ribs*
~
*Spiced Grilled
Sweet Potatoes
(p.170)*
~
*Chickpea &
Tomato Salad
(p195)*

1 Preheat the barbecue grill to medium indirect heat. Combine all the ingredients, except the butter and spare ribs in a medium saucepan. Bring to the boil, stirring to dissolve the sugar. You may want to have a lid handy to protect yourself and your kitchen from any sputtering. Reduce the heat and simmer for 25 minutes, stirring occasionally. With a whisk, blend in the butter cubes, a couple at a time, until incorporated. Set aside until needed.

2 Cook the ribs on the barbecue for 1-1¼ hours, turning once halfway through cooking time, until very tender. Brush generously with the sauce during the last 10 minutes of cooking time.

3 Remove from the barbecue and leave to rest for 10 minutes. Carve into individual ribs and serve immediately with extra sauce.

Bacon Cheeseburgers

Serves 4

800g minced beef (not too lean)
Salt and freshly ground black pepper
4–6 rindless lean back bacon rashers,
   cut in half
4 slices Cheddar cheese
4 sesame buns, split and toasted
Lettuce leaves
Sliced onion, mayonnaise, tomato
   ketchup and pickles, to taste

Menu

Bacon
Cheeseburgers
~
Tomato Salsa (p.162)
~
Old-fashioned
English Chips (p.164)
~
Berry Ice Lollies
(p.214)

1 Gently break the beef apart in a bowl with a fork. Season with salt and pepper, and shape into 4 large patties. Chill until ready to cook.

2 Put the bacon rashers in a heavy-based frying pan and cook over a medium heat for about 6 minutes, or until crisp and browned, turning once. Drain on kitchen paper.

3 Pour off all but 2 tablespoons of the bacon fat and add the burgers to the pan. Cook until browned and juicy, turning once. Allow 6 minutes for rare or 7–8 minutes for a well-done burger. Just before the burgers are ready, top each with a slice of cheese and cook until the cheese begins to soften.

4 Arrange a lettuce leaf on the bottom of each bun, then place a burger on top. Add the bacon and a selection of condiments. Cover with the bun top and serve with tomato salsa and chips.

Beef & Onion Pies

Serves 4

4 tablespoons vegetable oil
2 large onions, sliced
1 teaspoon brown sugar
675g lean rump steak, cubed
2 tablespoons plain flour
1 carrot, finely chopped
2 cloves garlic, finely chopped
225g baby button or baby chestnut
    mushrooms
150ml beef stock
150ml stout
1 tablespoon tomato purée
1 tablespoon Worcestershire sauce
1 tablespoon fresh thyme leaves
1 bay leaf
350g potatoes, peeled and cubed
300g ready-made puff pastry
1 egg, beaten

1 Heat half the oil in a large frying pan. Add the onions and cook for 5-7 minutes over medium heat until lightly golden. Stir in the sugar and cook for 4-5 minutes until caramelized. Set aside.

2 Preheat the oven to 140°C/275°F/Gas mark 1. Toss the meat in the flour, shaking off and reserving any excess. Heat the remaining oil over a medium heat in a large casserole and add the meat. Cook for 5-7 minutes until brown. Add the carrot, garlic and mushrooms and cook for 3-4 minutes until softened. Stir in the rest of the flour. Gradually add the stock and stout.

3 Add the tomato purée, Worcestershire sauce, thyme and bay leaf. Bring to the boil, cover and cook in the oven for 1 hour. Add the potatoes and cook for 20 minutes until tender. Increase the oven temperature to 200°C/400°F/Gas mark 6. Spoon the steak mixture into 4 x 300ml individual ovenproof pie dishes. Top with the onions.

4 Roll the pastry out thinly and cut 4 ovals or rounds about 5cm wider than the pie dishes. From these, trim a 2.5cm wide strip. Wet the rims of the dishes and attach the pastry strips. Wet the pastry strips and attach the pastry lids. Seal and make a decorative edge. Decorate with trimmings.

5 Brush the pastry with beaten egg. Bake for 25 minutes until the pastry is risen and golden. Leave to cool slightly before serving.

Menu

Beef & Onion Pies
~
*Roasted Vegetables
with Pine Nuts
& Parmesan
(p.187)*
~
*Sticky Toffee Pudding
(p.225)*

Pasta Shells
Filled with Bolognese

Serves 4

3 tablespoons vegetable oil
1 onion, finely chopped
1 clove garlic, crushed
2 sticks celery, finely chopped
50g streaky bacon
750g minced beef
600g can chopped tomatoes
3 tablespoons tomato purée
1 teaspoon mixed dried herbs
400ml milk
Salt and freshly ground black pepper
500g large dried pasta shells
Freshly grated Parmesan cheese, to
  serve

1 Heat 2 tablespoons oil in a large saucepan. Add the onion, garlic and celery and cook for 10 minutes. Add the bacon and minced beef and cook, stirring, over a high heat for 3-4 minutes until the beef has browned.

2 Stir in the chopped tomatoes, tomato purée, herbs and 250ml milk. Cover and simmer the bolognese for 40 minutes.

3 Add the remaining milk and simmer for a further 45 minutes. Taste and season with salt and pepper. Add a little water or stock if the sauce becomes very thick during cooking.

4 Preheat the oven to 180°C/350°F/Gas mark 4. Cook the pasta in a large pan of boiling salted water according to the instructions on the packet. Drain and toss in the remaining oil. Leave to cool a little, then arrange the shells in a large baking dish and fill with the bolognese sauce. Cook in the oven for 15 minutes. Serve with grated Parmesan cheese.

Menu

*Pasta Shells
Filled with Bolognese*
~
Panzanella (p.198)
~
*Poached Pears
with Maple Syrup
& Pecans
(p.218)*

Beef Stew
with Herb Dumplings

Serves 6

55g plain flour

Salt and freshly ground black pepper, to taste

1.5kg chuck steak or other stewing beef, cut into 5cm cubes

About 4 tablespoons vegetable oil

2 large onions, thinly sliced

250ml fruity red wine

500ml beef stock or water

125ml tomato ketchup

2 cloves garlic, finely chopped

2 bay leaves

1 large bouquet garni

2–3 carrots, cut into 1cm pieces

450g butternut or acorn squash, cut into chunks

275g pearl onions, peeled

1–2 tablespoons chopped parsley, to garnish

For the herb dumplings

175g plain flour

1½ teaspoons baking powder

½ teaspoon salt

75g beef or vegetable suet, grated

3–4 tablespoons finely chopped mixed fresh herbs, such as parsley, thyme sage, dill and chives

4–6 tablespoons milk

1 Put the flour in a plastic bag and season with salt and pepper. Working in small batches, put a few cubes of beef in the bag, twist the bag closed and shake to coat the meat evenly. Transfer the meat to a plate and continue to coat the remainder.

2 Heat the oil in a large, heavy-based saucepan over a medium-high heat. Working in batches, brown the beef cubes evenly on all sides, about 7 minutes for each batch. Transfer to a plate and continue until all the beef is browned.

continued ...

Menu

Beef Stew with Herb Dumplings

~

Maple-baked Acorn Squash (p.189)

~

Broad Beans with Prosciutto (p.180)

3 Add a little more oil, if necessary, then add the sliced onions. Cook for about 5 minutes, stirring, until softened. If you like a thicker stew, sprinkle over any remaining flour and cook for about 2 minutes, stirring to scrape up any browned bits from the bottom of the pan. Gradually whisk in the wine, stock or water, ketchup, garlic, bay leaves and bouquet garni, and season to taste.

4 Bring to the boil, skimming off any foam that rises to the surface. Return the beef to the pan, reduce the heat to medium-low and simmer, covered, for 1½ –1¾ hours, stirring occasionally, until the meat is almost tender. After simmering for 1 hour, stir in the carrots; and, after 1¼ –1½ hours, stir in the butternut squash.

5 To prepare the dumplings, sift the flour, baking powder and salt into a large bowl. Stir in the suet, mixed herbs and a little pepper. Add the milk, little by little, stirring to make a soft dough.

6 Remove the bouquet garni from the stew and stir in the pearl onions. Using a large spoon, drop 8 large or 12 small balls of dumpling mixture into the stew. Simmer for about 20 minutes, covered, until the dumplings are puffed and slightly firm to the touch.

Easy Burritos

Serves 4–6

4–6 large flour tortillas

2–3 tablespoons vegetable oil

1 onion, coarsely chopped

1 red or green pepper, seeded and
  chopped

1 clove garlic, crushed

675g boneless pork loin or skinless,
  boneless chicken breast, thinly sliced

½ teaspoon crushed chillies, or to taste

½ teaspoon ground cumin

Salt and freshly ground black pepper

300g can sweetcorn kernels, drained

2 ripe tomatoes, chopped

Bottled taco sauce, sliced avocado,
  sliced red onion, shredded iceberg
  lettuce, grated Cheddar cheese,
  soured cream and chopped fresh
  coriander leaves, to serve

Menu

Easy Burritos
~
Mexican Pot Beans
(p.190)
~
*Old-fashioned
Cornbread
(p.210)*
~
*Tomato Salsa
(p.162)*

1 Preheat the oven to 180°C/350°F/Gas mark 4. Wrap the tortillas tightly in aluminium foil and heat in the oven for about 15 minutes.

2 Meanwhile, heat 2 tablespoons of oil in a large frying pan or wok over a medium-high heat. Add the onion, pepper and garlic and stir-fry 2–3 minutes until beginning to soften. Transfer to a plate and set aside.

3 Add the remaining oil, the pork or chicken, crushed chillies and cumin and stir-fry for about 3 minutes. Season with salt and pepper and return the cooked vegetables to the pan. Add the sweetcorn and tomatoes and cook 2–3 minutes longer until heated through.

4 Lay the warm tortillas on a surface and divide the mixture evenly among them, placing it near one edge. Top with the chosen accompaniments. Fold the edge nearest the filling over just enough to cover the filling. Fold the two sides over to form an envelope shape.

Roast Rib of Beef

with Caramelized Shallots

Serves 4

2.75kg rib of beef, bone in
2 tablespoons bacon fat or vegetable
 oil
Salt and freshly ground black pepper
6 fresh thyme sprigs
450g shallots, peeled and left whole
2 tablespoons granulated sugar

For the sauce
1 tablespoon plain flour
250ml red wine
500ml beef stock

1 Preheat the oven to 200°C/400°F/Gas mark 6.
Put the beef in a large roasting tin and spoon
over the bacon fat or oil. Season well with salt and
pepper and lay the thyme sprigs over the joint.
Roast in the oven for 1 hour.

2 Meanwhile, bring a saucepan of water to
the boil. Add the shallots and simmer for
15 minutes, then drain well.

3 Remove the beef
from the oven.
Arrange the shallots
around the beef.
Sprinkle the sugar
over the shallots
and return to the
oven for a further
30 minutes, basting and turning the shallots after
15 minutes. Transfer the beef and shallots to a warm
plate and leave to rest for at least 15 minutes.

4 For the sauce, pour off all but 2 tablespoons
of the bacon fat or oil from the roasting tin,
add the flour and cook on the hob for 1–2 minutes.
Add the wine, stirring well to prevent lumps, then
increase the heat a little and boil the liquid for
3–4 minutes to reduce and thicken.

5 Add the beef stock, reduce the heat and
simmer for 10 minutes. Taste and season with
salt and pepper.

> ### Menu
>
> *Roast Rib of Beef
> with Caramelized
> Shallots*
> ~
> *Leek & Potato
> Layer (p.169)*
> ~
> *Pumpkin Pie
> (p.220)*

Old-fashioned Meatloaf

Serves 6

2 tablespoons vegetable oil, plus extra
  for oiling
1 large onion, finely chopped
1 carrot, grated
2 cloves garlic, chopped
900g minced beef
75g fresh white breadcrumbs
2 eggs, lightly beaten
½ teaspoon dried thyme
2–4 tablespoons finely chopped
  parsley
1 tablespoon Worcestershire sauce
150ml tomato ketchup, plus extra for
  glazing
Salt and freshly ground black pepper

1 Heat the oil in a frying pan. Add the onion and carrot and cook for about 5 minutes, stirring frequently, until the vegetables begin to soften. Stir in the garlic and cook for a further 1 minute. Remove from the heat and leave to cool.

2 Preheat the oven to 180°C/350°F/Gas mark 4 and lightly oil a 23 x 13 x 7.5cm loaf tin. Combine the beef, breadcrumbs and cooled vegetable mixture in a large bowl. Add the eggs, thyme, parsley, Worcestershire sauce, ketchup and salt and pepper, then use a fork or your hands to mix the ingredients lightly together until just blended. Do not overwork the mixture or the meatloaf will be too compact and dry.

3 Spoon the mixture into the prepared tin, pressing gently to smooth the top. Bake for about 1¼ hours, or until the edges begin to shrink from the sides of the tin. About 10 minutes before the meatloaf is done, brush the top with about 2 tablespoons ketchup to give it a glaze.

4 Set aside to cool for about 10 minutes, covered loosely with foil. Pour off any excess juices, if you like, before leaving the meatloaf to cool. To serve, turn out on to a dish or plate and cut into slices. Alternatively, slice the meatloaf from the tin.

Menu

Old-fashioned
Meatloaf
~
Succotash
(p.173)
~
Texas Pilaf
(p.203)
~
Apple Cake Bars
(p.241)

Beef Stew with Star Anise

Serves 4-6

3 tablespoons vegetable oil

2 cloves garlic, crushed

2.5cm fresh root ginger, peeled and finely chopped

3 onions, finely sliced

900g boneless beef (sirloin), cut into 2.5cm cubes

3 tablespoons hoisin sauce

3 tablespoons light soy sauce

4 whole star anise

1 tablespoon mild honey or sugar

2 tablespoons rice wine or sherry

4 carrots, peeled and cut into 2.5cm slices on the diagonal

Salt and freshly ground black pepper

1 tablespoon fresh chopped coriander, to garnish

Steamed pak choi and rice, to serve

Menu

Beef Stew with Star Anise

~

New England Blueberry Pancakes (p.226)

1 Heat the oil in a heavy-based frying pan or casserole. Add the garlic, ginger and onions and sauté over a high heat until golden brown.

2 Add the beef and brown on all sides. Pour over enough water to cover and stir in the hoisin and soy sauces, the star anise, honey or sugar and rice wine or sherry. Simmer for 1½ hours, stirring from time to time to prevent sticking. Check the liquid level, adding more water if necessary.

3 Add the carrots and cook for a further 30 minutes, or until the meat and carrots are tender. Season to taste with salt and pepper.

4 Transfer to a serving dish, garnish with chopped coriander, and serve with steamed pak choi and rice.

Braised Lamb Shanks

with Mirepoix Vegetables

Serves 4

1 tablespoon olive oil
4 lamb shanks
2 carrots, cut into very fine strips
3 sticks celery, cut into very fine strips
1 large onion, finely chopped
2 cloves garlic, finely chopped
450ml red wine
225ml lamb or chicken stock
1 tablespoon tomato purée
2 bay leaves
2 fresh rosemary sprigs
Salt and freshly ground black pepper

Tip

Mirepoix vegetables – diced carrot, onion and celery – are perfect for enhancing soups, stews and stock.

1 Preheat the oven to 150°C/300°F/ Gas mark 2. Heat the oil in a large casserole and brown the lamb shanks all over for about 10 minutes. Transfer to a plate.

Menu

Braised Lamb Shanks with Mirepoix Vegetables

~

Duchesse Potatoes (p.166)

~

Stove-top Rice Pudding with Dried Fruit (p.245)

2 Add the vegetables to the casserole and fry for about 15 minutes until they start to take on a little colour. Return the lamb shanks to the casserole and pour the wine and stock over them. Add the tomato purée, bay leaves and rosemary and season well with salt and pepper.

3 Bring to the boil, cover with a lid and cook in the oven for 3-3½ hours. Turn the meat occasionally during cooking.

Tagine
with Prunes & Almonds

Serves 6

Menu

Tagine with Prunes &
Almonds
~
Chickpea & Tomato
Salad (p.195)
~
Spiced Baked Apples
(p.224)

1.3kg boneless lean lamb, cut into 4cm
  cubes
4 tablespoons ras el hanout or curry
  spice mix
120ml water
120ml olive oil
4 onions, halved and sliced
3 cinnamon sticks
1 large white turnip, cut into 1cm
  slices
350g prunes
3 cloves garlic, crushed
Salt and freshly ground black pepper
200g toasted whole blanched almonds
2 tablespoons fresh chopped coriander
  or parsley, to garnish
Steamed couscous, to serve

1 Put the lamb in a large non-metallic bowl.
Blend the ras el hanout with the water and pour
over the lamb. Mix well to coat each piece of meat.
Marinate for at least 3 hours in the refrigerator.

2 Heat the oil in a heavy-based frying pan or casserole. Add the onions and sauté over a high heat until they start to brown. Add the meat and cook until the pieces are brown on all sides.

3 Pour over enough water to cover, then add the cinnamon sticks and turnip. Simmer uncovered, for 30 minutes, stirring occasionally so that the meat doesn't stick to the bottom of the pan. Add more water if necessary.

4 Stir in the prunes and garlic, cover the pan and simmer for 30 minutes until the meat is tender, stirring from time to time.

5 Season with salt and pepper. Sprinkle toasted almonds over the top, garnish with coriander or parsley, and serve with steamed couscous.

Lamb Meatballs
with Buttermilk & Herb Dip

Makes about 40

3 tablespoons vegetable oil, plus extra
   for frying
2 onions, finely chopped
4 cloves garlic, crushed
2 tablespoons paprika
2 teaspoons dried thyme
2 teaspoons cinnamon
900g minced lamb
2 tablespoons finely chopped fresh
   coriander
Salt and freshly ground black pepper

For the buttermilk dip
300ml buttermilk
1 teaspoon chopped fresh thyme
1 tablespoon chopped fresh chives

1 Heat the oil in a large frying pan. Add the onions and garlic and cook for 10 minutes. Add the paprika, thyme and cinnamon and cook for a further 1-2 minutes. Leave to cool completely.

2 Mix the onion mixture into the lamb, then add the coriander, and season well with salt and pepper. (To test the level of seasoning, cook just a nugget of the mixture.)

Menu

*Lamb Meatballs with
Buttermilk & Herb Dip*
~
Waldorf Salad (p.196)
~
*Bacon & Caramelized
Onion Rolls (p.211)*
~
*Meringues with Cream
& Blueberries (p.223)*

3 Shape the mixture into 40 small meatballs. Heat a little oil in a large frying pan and cook the meatballs for 10-12 minutes, turning them halfway through cooking.

4 For the dip, mix the buttermilk and herbs together in a bowl. Taste and season with salt and pepper.

5 Serve the meatballs warm with cocktail sticks for your guests to dunk the meatballs into the buttermilk dip.

Papaya Lamb Kebabs

Serves 6

900g boneless lamb, cut into 2.5cm
  cubes
12 pearl onions
2 green peppers, cored, seeded and cut
  into 2.5cm squares
1 red pepper, cored, seeded and cut
  into 2.5cm squares
Salt and freshly ground black pepper

For the marinade
1 small ripe papaya
Juice of 2 limes
1 teaspoon garam masala
1 teaspoon ground coriander
2 tablespoons light olive oil
60ml natural yoghurt

Menu

*Papaya
Lamb Kebabs*
~
*Stir-fried Brown
Rice & Vegetables
(p.202)*

1 Make the marinade. Cut the papaya in half,
spoon out and discard the black seeds, then
scrape the flesh into a blender or food processor.
Add the remaining ingredients and process until
smooth. Spoon into a shallow glass dish, add the
lamb cubes and mix well. Cover and leave to
marinate for 2-3 hours, stirring occasionally.

2 Preheat the grill to medium. Put the unpeeled
onions in a saucepan and pour over enough
cold water to cover. Bring to the boil and boil for
4 minutes, then drain. When cool enough to handle,
slip off the skins.

3 Drain the lamb cubes, reserving the marinade.
Thread them on to 12 metal skewers,
alternating them with the onions and pepper
squares. Season well with salt and pepper.

4 Cook the kebabs under the grill or on the
barbecue for 15-20 minutes, turning them
occasionally and basting them with the marinade.

Kofta

Serves 6

450g minced beef
450g minced lamb
2 onions, finely chopped
1 tablespoon paprika
1 tablespoon coriander seeds
1 teaspoon salt
1/2 teaspoon freshly ground black pepper
1 egg
50g fresh breadcrumbs
3 tablespoons water
Butter, for greasing

For the tomato sauce

3 tablespoons olive oil
1 onion, finely chopped
6 ripe tomatoes, skinned, seeded and
   chopped
1 tablespoon ras el hanout or curry
   spice mix
1 teaspoon ground cumin
1 teaspoon coriander seeds
1 cinnamon stick
1 teaspoon sugar
120ml water
Salt and freshly ground black pepper
2 tablespoons toasted sesame seeds,
   to garnish

Menu

Kofta
~
Spiced Courgettes
(p.185)
~
Chilled Mandarin
& Lemon Mousse
(p.233)

1 Mix the beef and lamb together in a large bowl. Add the onions, paprika, coriander seeds, salt and pepper. Stir in the egg, breadcrumbs and the 3 tablespoons water until well mixed. Chill for about 3 hours.

2 Preheat the oven to 220°C/425°F/Gas mark 7. Grease a baking dish.

3 Shape spoonfuls of the meat mixture into walnut-sized balls, and arrange in the baking dish. Bake for 15 minutes, or until lightly browned.

4 To make the tomato sauce, heat the oil in a large saucepan. Add the onions and cook over a high heat until transparent. Add the tomatoes, ras el hanout, spices and sugar, and stir in the 120ml water. Simmer for 20 minutes. Add 2 teaspoons salt and 1/2 teaspoon pepper.

5 Add the meatballs and any juices to the sauce and simmer gently for about 30 minutes. Remove the cinnamon stick and adjust the seasoning. Transfer to a serving dish. Sprinkle with toasted sesame seeds.

Roast Leg of Lamb

Serves 6–8

1 leg of lamb (weigh once prepared for
  cooking)
2–3 cloves garlic, sliced
2–3 fresh rosemary sprigs
Salt and freshly ground black pepper
250ml red wine
300ml lamb stock or water

1 Preheat the oven to 220°C/425°F/Gas mark 7.
Using a small, sharp knife, make about 8-10 deep
incisions in the meat. Into each incision, insert a slice
of garlic along with a few leaves of rosemary (you
can usually pull off small bunches of leaves attached
at the stem end). Season the lamb well all over with
salt and pepper. Transfer to a large roasting tin.

2 Roast the lamb for 25 minutes per 450g plus
25 minutes for medium, 30 minutes per 450g
plus 30 minutes for well done. When finished,
remove the meat from the roasting tin to a carving
board. Leave to rest for 10-15 minutes.

3 To make the gravy, remove as much fat as
possible from the roasting tin, using a metal
spoon. Place the tin on the hob over a medium
heat. When sizzling, pour in the red wine. Using a
spoon or whisk, scrape up any residue in the
bottom of the tin.
Allow the wine to
simmer rapidly until
reduced to a syrupy
consistency. Now
add the stock or
water (if you have
any water from
cooking vegetables
or potatoes, use
that). Bring to the
boil and simmer
rapidly until reduced by about half. Taste and add a
little seasoning. If the flavour is not concentrated
enough, continue reducing a little more. Strain the
gravy into a jug or gravy boat. Slice the meat and
serve with the gravy.

Menu

Roast Leg of Lamb
~
*Provençal
Ratatouille (p.155)*
~
*Luxury Mashed
Potatoes (p.166)*
~
*Double-crust Apple Pie
(p.228)*

Baked Lasagne

Serves 8

2 tablespoons olive oil
1 onion, finely chopped
2 cloves garlic, crushed
450g minced beef
840g can plum tomatoes
450g can tomato sauce or passata
2–3 tablespoons tomato purée
Salt and freshly ground black pepper
1 tablespoon chopped fresh oregano
1 tablespoon chopped fresh thyme
1 teaspoon crushed red chillies
1 bay leaf
About 14 fresh or dried lasagne sheets
2 eggs, lightly beaten
450g ricotta cheese
2 tablespoons chopped fresh parsley
   or basil
450g mozzarella cheese
Freshly grated Parmesan cheese

Menu

Baked Lasagne
~
*Roasted Tomato &
Goat's Cheese Salad
(p.200)*
~
*Chocolate Mousse
(p.232)*

1 Heat the oil in a large saucepan over a medium heat. Add the onion and cook until just soft. Add the garlic and beef and cook until browned. Stir in the tomatoes, tomato sauce or passata and tomato purée, then season. Add the oregano, thyme, chillies and bay leaf. Bring to the boil (squash the tomatoes to break them up.) Reduce the heat to low, partially cover and simmer for 45 minutes, stirring occasionally, until the sauce is slightly reduced. Remove the bay leaf.

2 For fresh lasagne, no pre-cooking is necessary. For dried lasagne, bring a large, deep frying pan half-filled with salted water to the boil over a high heat. Working in batches, cook the lasagne for 2–3 minutes. Drain and lay out to dry on a tea towel.

3 Preheat the oven to 190°C/375°F/Gas mark 5. Beat the eggs and ricotta together in a bowl until blended, season and stir in the parsley or basil.

4 Spoon enough meat sauce into a deep baking dish about 23 x 33cm just to cover the bottom. Cover with a layer of lasagne. Spread a third of the ricotta mixture on top and sprinkle with a little mozzarella, then cover with a layer of meat sauce. Continue the layers, ending with meat sauce and mozzarella. Sprinkle with grated Parmesan. Transfer the dish to a baking tray and bake for 45–55 minutes, or until bubbling and crisp around the edges. Leave to stand for 5–10 minutes before serving.

FISH

- Home-smoked Salmon
- Atlantic Spiced Salmon with New Potato & Spring Onion Salad
- New England Clam Chowder
- Fish & Chips
- Crab Louis
- Swordfish Kebabs with Lemon Herb Mayonnaise
- Fish Caldine
- Beer-battered Prawns
- Grapefruit, Prawn & Avocado Salad
- Prawn Jambalaya
- Marinated Prawns with Dill Mayonnaise
- Poached Whole Salmon
- Thai Green Curry

- Bream with Garlic & Coriander Butter
- Crispy Fish Cakes
- Sweet Chilli Salmon
- Tuna Noodle Casserole
- Tuna Melts
- Grilled Tuna with Warm Bean Salad
- Baked Fish with Celeriac
- Fish Finger Sandwiches with Mayonnaise
- Roast Cod with Fried Gremolata Breadcrumbs
- New England Fishballs
- Smoked Trout Terrine with Cucumber Salad
- Harissa-coated Monkfish

CHAPTER THREE

FISH

Home-smoked Salmon

Serves 6

175g rice
8 fresh rosemary sprigs
Six 175g salmon fillets
2 teaspoons vegetable oil
Salt and freshly ground black pepper

Menu

*Home-smoked
Salmon*

~

*Roast Peppers
with Mozzarella
(p.154)*

~

*New England
Blueberry Pancakes
(p.226)*

1 Preheat the oven to 200°C/400°F/Gas mark 6.
Line a wok with aluminium foil and pour in the
rice. Arrange the rosemary on top of the rice.
Sprinkle with a little water and fit a round wire
rack in the wok. Heat the wok until smoking, then
put the salmon fillets on the wire rack. Cover
tightly and smoke for 5 minutes.

2 Remove the salmon to a roasting tin and brush
it with oil. Season with salt and pepper and
cook in the oven for 5 minutes. Rest for a few
minutes and serve the salmon warm.

Atlantic Spiced Salmon
with New Potato & Spring Onion Salad

Serves 8

8 Atlantic salmon fillets,
   about 225g each
4 tablespoons paprika
4 tablespoons dried oregano
2 cloves garlic, crushed
½ teaspoon cayenne pepper
8 tablespoons olive oil
Salt and freshly ground black pepper

For the salad
2kg new potatoes, scrubbed
10 tablespoons vegetable oil
2 tablespoons lemon juice
15 spring onions, finely chopped
4 tablespoons chopped fresh mint

1 Put the salmon fillets in a large non-metallic dish. Mix the paprika, oregano, garlic, cayenne, olive oil, and a few grinds of pepper together in a large bowl. Pour the marinade over the salmon and work it into the flesh with your hands. Leave to marinate in the refrigerator for 2 hours.

2 Meanwhile, for the salad, cook the new potatoes in a saucepan of boiling salted water until tender. Mix the oil and lemon juice together in a bowl. Drain the potatoes, then return them to the pan and pour the dressing over. Toss well, then cover and leave the potatoes to steep in the dressing for 30 minutes.

3 Preheat the oven to 220°C/425°F/Gas mark 7. Put the salmon in a large roasting tin, season well with salt and roast in the oven for 12–15 minutes. Set aside for 5 minutes before serving.

4 Transfer the potatoes to a serving dish and stir in the onions and mint, then serve with the salmon.

Menu

Atlantic Spiced
Salmon with New
Potato & Spring
Onion Salad
~
Sticky Toffee
Pudding
(p.225)

New England
Clam Chowder

Serves 4

Menu

New England
Clam Chowder

~

Bacon &
Caramelized
Onion Rolls
(p.211)

1.5kg fresh clams
25g butter
1 onion, finely chopped
3 bacon rashers, finely chopped
2 medium-sized potatoes, peeled and
   diced
4 fresh thyme sprigs
1 bay leaf
600ml milk
Salt and freshly ground black pepper

Tip

Served with hot crusty
bread and followed by fruit
or cheese, this will make
a meal in itself for lunch
or supper.

1 Wash and scrub the clams. Discard any that refuse to close after a sharp tap. Pour enough water to come up to 1cm in a large saucepan and add the clams. Cover with a tight-fitting lid and bring to the boil. Cook for 2 minutes then drain, reserving 300ml of the cooking liquid. Remove the clams from their shells, discarding any that are shut.

2 Melt the butter in a large saucepan. Add the onion, bacon and potatoes and fry for 5 minutes.

3 Add the thyme sprigs, bay leaf and milk. Pour in the reserved liquid and simmer the soup until the potatoes are on the point of breaking up, about 20–25 minutes. Remove the thyme and bay leaf. Season well with salt and pepper and stir in the clams. Simmer for 1 minute, to heat the soup through and serve.

Fish & Chips

Serves 6–8

15g fresh yeast
300ml beer
225g plain flour
2 teaspoons salt
900g old potatoes
Vegetable oil, for deep-frying
4 thick pieces cod fillet, about 175g
  each, preferably from the head end
Salt and freshly ground black pepper
Fresh parsley sprigs, to garnish

1 For the batter, cream the yeast with a little of the beer to a smooth paste. Gradually stir in the rest of the beer. Sift the flour and salt into a bowl, make a well in the centre and add the yeast mixture. Gradually whisk to a smooth batter. Cover and leave at room temperature for 1 hour until foamy and thick.

2 For the chips, cut the potatoes into chips about 1cm thick. Heat a large saucepan half filled with oil for deep-frying to 140°C/275°F, or until a cube of bread browns in 1 minute. Cook the chips in two batches for about 5 minutes, or until they are cooked through but not browned. Drain on kitchen paper and set aside.

3 Increase the heat to 170°C/325°F, or until a cube of bread browns in 45 seconds. Season the fish generously with salt and pepper and then dip into the batter. Deep-fry two pieces at a time for 7-8 minutes until deep golden brown and the fish is cooked through. Lift out, drain on kitchen paper and keep warm while you cook the remaining fish pieces. Keep the fish warm while you finish the chips.

4 Increase the heat to 190°C/375°F, or until a cube of bread browns in 30 seconds. Fry the chips again, in two batches, for 2–3 minutes until crisp and golden. Drain on kitchen paper and sprinkle with salt. Garnish the fish and chips with parsley sprigs, and serve with lemon wedges and mayonnaise.

Menu

Fish & Chips
~
*Caramel
Ice Cream (p.217)*

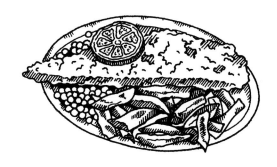

Crab Louis

Serves 4

1 head soft or butterhead lettuce,
  leaves separated, washed and dried
450–675g white crabmeat, picked over
4 hard-boiled eggs, halved
8 cherry tomatoes, halved
20 black olives, preferably niçoise or
  herb-dried
1 tablespoon chopped fresh dill, to
  garnish

For the dressing
225g mayonnaise
1 tablespoon lemon juice
½ small onion, grated
½ green pepper, seeded
  and finely chopped
60ml sweet or hot chilli sauce, or
  to taste
1 teaspoon Worcestershire sauce

Menu

Crab Louis
~
Spanish Omelette
(p.136)
~
Chocolate Mousse
(p.232)

1 To make the dressing, put the mayonnaise in a bowl and stir in the lemon juice, onion, pepper, chilli and Worcestershire sauces until well blended. Set aside.

2 Arrange the lettuce leaves on 4 plates. Mound equal amounts of crabmeat in the middle and arrange the hard-boiled eggs and tomato halves around the crab.

3 Sprinkle the olives over the top and spoon over some of the dressing. Sprinkle with dill to garnish and serve the remaining dressing separately.

Swordfish Kebabs with

Lemon Herb Mayonnaise

Serves 4

For the mayonnaise
1 egg yolk
Salt and freshly ground black pepper
1 tablespoon white wine vinegar
½ teaspoon Dijon mustard
200ml groundnut or light olive oil

For the flavouring
2 teaspoons grated lemon zest
1 tablespoon chopped fresh tarragon
1 tablespoon chopped capers
1 tablespoon chopped fresh parsley

For the kebabs
450g swordfish steaks, cut into bite-
    sized pieces
2 red onions, cut into 6 wedges
2 limes, each cut into wedges
2 tablespoons olive oil
Pared zest of 1 lime
1 teaspoon fresh thyme leaves
2 tablespoons maple syrup
Boiled new potatoes, to serve

1 For the mayonnaise, whisk the egg yolk, salt and pepper, vinegar and mustard together until they thicken slightly.

2 Add the groundnut oil a drop at a time whisking continuously. When the sauce begins to thicken and lighten, start adding the oil in a thin, steady stream, whisking continuously.

3 When all the oil has been added, taste for seasoning then stir in the lemon zest, tarragon, capers and parsley. Set aside.

4 Put the swordfish, red onion and lime wedges into a bowl and toss in the olive oil, lime zest, thyme leaves and maple syrup. Chill 2-3 hours.

5 Preheat the grill. Thread the fish, lime wedges and red onion onto 8 skewers and cook under the hot grill for 5-6 minutes, turning often until starting to colour on the outside. Serve the kebabs with a spoonful of the sauce and boiled new potatoes.

> **Menu**
>
> *Swordfish
> Kebabs with Lemon
> Herb Mayonnaise*
> ~
> *Classic Healthy
> Coleslaw
> (p. 191)*

Fish Caldine

Serves 4–6

2.5cm fresh root ginger, peeled
1 teaspoon ground cumin
1 teaspoon ground turmeric
1 clove garlic, peeled
Salt
400ml can unsweetened coconut milk
4 tablespoons vegetable oil
900g firm-fleshed white fish, either
  whole or in fillets (scored three times
  on each side if using whole fish)
1 onion, finely chopped
1 fresh green chilli, finely chopped
1 tablespoon whole fresh coriander
  leaves
1 chilli, sliced lengthways, to garnish
1 lime, cut into wedges, to serve

Menu

Fish Caldine

~

Braised Fennel
(p.177)

~

Latkes
(p.171)

~

Cherry Clafoutis
(p.243)

1 Put the ginger, cumin, turmeric, garlic and 1 teaspoon salt in a food processor and process to a smooth purée. With the motor running, add the coconut milk and process until smooth. Set aside.

2 Heat half the oil in a heavy-based frying pan. Add the fish and sear for 2 minutes on each side. Carefully remove the fish and set aside. In the same pan, add the remaining oil and fry the onion and finely chopped chilli together over a high heat until the onion is soft and transparent. Return the fish to the pan. Add the coconut milk mixture and reduce the heat.

3 Simmer gently for 10–15 minutes, basting the fish with the coconut mixture frequently, until most of the liquid has been absorbed. Adjust the seasoning.

4 Transfer the fish to a serving dish and sprinkle with coriander leaves. Garnish with sliced green chilli and serve with lime wedges for squeezing over.

Beer-battered Prawns

Serves 4–6

675–900g large raw prawns, peeled and
deveined, with tails if possible
Vegetable oil, for deep-frying

For the batter
120g plain flour
1½ teaspoons salt
185–250ml beer
Lemon and lime wedges and fresh
parsley sprigs, to garnish

Menu

*Beer-battered
Prawns*

~

*Old-fashioned
English Chips
(p.164)*

1 Rinse the prawns and dry them well with
kitchen paper.

2 For the batter, sift the flour into a bowl and stir
in the salt. Using a fork, gradually stir in the
beer – do not overmix the batter as a few lumps of
flour will not matter.

3 Heat the oil for deep-frying to 190°C/375°F
over a medium-high heat. Using your fingers or
tongs and working in batches, dip the prawns into
the batter and then drop them into the hot oil.
Cook for about 1 minute, until crisp and golden,
turning once. Drain on kitchen paper and keep hot
until all the prawns are battered and cooked.

4 Arrange the prawns in a napkin-lined basket
or bowl and garnish with lemon and lime
wedges and parsley sprigs.

Grapefruit, Prawn & Avocado Salad

Serves 4

1 clove garlic, peeled
Grated zest and juice of 1 lemon
2 tablespoons olive oil
450g raw peeled prawns
2 grapefruit
2 avocados
Small bunch of fresh chives

Menu

Grapefruit,
Prawn & Avocado
Salad
~
Onion Quiche
(p.139)
~
Chocolate-covered
Doughnuts
(p.238)

Tip

To stop a cut avocado from discolouring, brush the cut surfaces with lemon juice.

1 Pound the garlic in a mortar and pestle with the lemon zest and juice and 1 tablespoon of the oil. Spoon into a bowl and add the prawns. Stir and leave to marinate for 30 minutes.

2 Peel and segment the grapefruit with a serrated fruit knife and arrange in a salad bowl. Halve the avocados, remove the stones and peel away the skin. Thinly slice and carefully arrange among the grapefruit segments.

3 Heat the remaining oil in a frying pan. Add the prawns, and fry for 3-4 minutes until firm and pink all over. Leave to cool then spoon over the salad. Snip the chives with a pair of kitchen scissors and scatter over the salad. Chill until ready to serve.

Prawn Jambalaya

Serves 6

2 tablespoons vegetable oil

2 medium onions, roughly chopped

1 green pepper, seeded and roughly chopped

2 sticks celery, roughly chopped

3 cloves garlic, finely chopped

2 teaspoons paprika

300g skinless, boneless chicken breasts, chopped

100g chorizo sausage, chopped

3 large tomatoes, skinned and chopped

450g long-grain rice

900ml hot chicken or fish stock

1 teaspoon dried oregano

2 fresh bay leaves

12 large prawn tails

4 spring onions, finely chopped

2 tablespoons chopped fresh parsley

Salt and freshly ground black pepper

1 Heat the oil in a large frying pan. Add the onions, pepper, celery and garlic and cook for 8-10 minutes until all the vegetables have softened. Add the paprika and cook for a further 30 seconds. Add the chicken and sausage and cook for 8-10 minutes until lightly browned. Add the tomatoes to the pan. Cook for 2-3 minutes until collapsed.

2 Add the rice to the pan and stir well. Pour in the hot stock, oregano and bay leaves and stir well. Cover and simmer for 10 minutes over a very low heat.

3 Add the prawns and stir well. Cover again and cook for a further 6-8 minutes until the rice is tender and the prawns are cooked through.

4 Stir in the spring onions, parsley and season to taste with salt and pepper. Serve immediately.

Menu

Prawn Jambalaya

~

Spinach with Paneer (p.151)

~

Apple Sauce Sundae (p.236)

Marinated Prawns
with Dill Mayonnaise

Menu

Marinated Prawns with Dill Mayonnaise

~

Parsley & Leek Frittata (p.135)

~

Peanut Butter Brownies (p.240)

Serves 8

40 large raw peeled prawns
2 cloves garlic, crushed
Juice and grated zest of 2 limes
1 red chilli, seeded and very finely chopped

For the dill mayonnaise
2 egg yolks
1 teaspoon mustard powder
2 teaspoons white wine vinegar
Pinch of salt
250ml groundnut or vegetable oil
2 teaspoons soured cream
1 tablespoon chopped fresh dill

1 Put the prawns in a shallow, non-metallic dish. Mix the garlic, lime juice, zest and chilli together in a bowl. Pour the marinade over the prawns. Mix well and leave to marinate for 1 hour.

2 To make the mayonnaise, put the egg yolks, mustard powder, vinegar and salt in a mixing bowl. Using an electric whisk, beat in the oil, drop by drop at first. When half of the oil has been added, pour in the remaining oil in a thin, steady stream, whisking continuously. If the mayonnaise becomes very thick, dilute with 1 tablespoon warm water.

3 Stir the soured cream and dill into the mayonnaise. Leave to chill until ready to serve.

4 Put the prawns in a steamer (you may need to do this in batches) and steam for 3–4 minutes until they turn pink and firm. Serve chilled or at room temperature with the dill mayonnaise.

Poached Whole Salmon

Serves 8–10

2 carrots, sliced
2 leeks, sliced
2 medium onions, sliced
1 teaspoon black peppercorns
1 bouquet garni
500ml dry white wine
2 teaspoons white wine vinegar
500ml cold water
1 whole salmon, about 2kg in weight,
   scaled and washed
Boiled new potatoes, to serve

1 To make the court-bouillon, put the carrots, leeks, onions, peppercorns, bouquet garni, wine and wine vinegar into a large saucepan along with the water. Bring slowly to the boil and simmer gently for 20 minutes. Remove from the heat and leave to cool.

2 Put the salmon into a fish kettle or large saucepan. Pour over the court-bouillon, adding water if necessary to cover the fish. Bring slowly up to a simmer and cook for 15 minutes. Remove from the heat and leave in the liquid until cold.

3 Lift the fish from the poaching liquid and on to a large chopping board. Remove the fish head and discard. Carefully remove the skin from the uppermost section of the fish. Slide a knife between the spine and bones to remove the fillet in one piece if possible. Remove the bones and replace the fillet.

4 Carefully flip the fish and repeat, first removing the skin, then the fillet. You now have a boneless cooked salmon. Carefully transfer to a serving platter. Serve with mayonnaise and boiled new potatoes.

Menu

*Poached
Whole Salmon*
~
*Spinach Roulade
(p.157)*
~
*Boston Cream Pie
(p.244)*

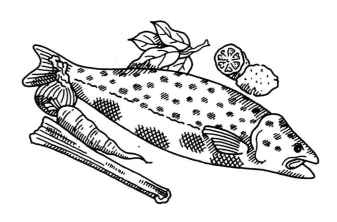

Thai Green Curry

Serves 4

For the green curry paste

5 fresh green chillies, seeded and chopped

2 teaspoons fresh lemon grass, chopped

1 large shallot, chopped

2 cloves garlic, chopped

1 teaspoon freshly grated ginger or galangal, if available

2 coriander roots, chopped

½ teaspoon ground coriander

¼ teaspoon ground cumin

1 kaffir lime leaf, finely chopped

1 teaspoon shrimp paste (optional)

½ teaspoon salt

2 tablespoons vegetable oil

1 clove garlic, chopped

1 small aubergine, diced

120ml coconut cream

2 tablespoons Thai fish sauce

1 teaspoon sugar

500g raw peeled tiger prawns

120ml fish stock

2 kaffir lime leaves, finely shredded

About 15 Thai basil leaves, or ordinary basil

1 To make the green curry paste, put all the ingredients into a blender or spice grinder and process to a fairly smooth paste, adding a little water if necessary. Alternatively, pound the ingredients using a mortar and pestle until fairly smooth. Set aside.

2 To make the curry, heat the oil in a frying pan or wok until almost smoking and add the garlic. Fry until golden. Add the green curry paste that you have made and stir-fry a few seconds before adding the aubergine. Stir-fry for about 4–5 minutes until softened.

3 Add the coconut cream. Bring to the boil and stir until the cream thickens and curdles slightly. Add the fish sauce and sugar and stir well until combined.

4 Add the prawns and stock. Simmer for 3–4 minutes, stirring occasionally, until the prawns are just tender. Add the lime leaves and basil leaves and cook for a further minute.

Menu

*Thai
Green Curry*
~
*Coconut Rice
(p.206)*
~
*Mango
Ice Cream
(p.216)*

Bream with Garlic

& Coriander Butter

Serves 4

1 tablespoon brown sugar
1 teaspoon freshly ground black
  pepper
1 teaspoon salt
4 small bream or 2 large bream, about
  1.75kg total weight
120g unsalted butter, softened
2 cloves garlic, crushed
2 tablespoons chopped fresh coriander
Juice and finely grated zest of 1 lemon
1 tablespoon hot chilli flakes, such as
  jalapeño
Salt and freshly ground black pepper
Lemon wedges, to serve

1 Preheat the barbecue grill to high direct heat.
Mix the brown sugar, black pepper and salt
together. Rub the mixture into the skin of the fish.
Set aside.

2 Beat the butter, garlic, coriander, lemon zest and
chilli flakes together in a medium mixing bowl.
Season to taste with salt and pepper. When
thoroughly mixed, add the lemon juice and beat
until incorporated.
Scrape the mixture
on to a large piece of
greaseproof paper
and, using the paper
to help you, shape
into a log. Enclose
the butter in the
paper and twist the
ends together to seal. Chill in the refrigerator
until needed.

3 Cook the fish over high direct heat for
8-12 minutes, turning once halfway through
the cooking time, until the skin is crisp and golden
and the flesh just flakes. Remove from the heat and
transfer to serving plates (if using small bream) or
cut into fillets (if using larger fish).

4 Slice the butter thickly and put 1-2 slices on
top of the fish. Serve immediately with the
wedges of lemon.

Menu

Bream with
Garlic & Coriander
Butter
~
Spinach Roulade
(p.157)
~
Pumpkin Pie
(p.220)

Crispy Fish Cakes

Serves 4

Juice of ½ lemon
675g cod or other white fish, salmon
   or trout fillets or steaks
450g potatoes, cut into pieces
Salt and freshly ground black pepper
75g butter
1 onion, finely chopped
1 large egg
1 egg yolk
2 tablespoons chopped fresh dill,
   chives or parsley, or a mixture
Dried breadcrumbs, for coating
Vegetable oil, for frying
Fresh parsley or dill sprigs, to garnish

1 Bring a medium frying pan half-filled with water to the boil. Add the lemon juice and 1 teaspoon salt. Add the fish and reduce the heat to low. Simmer until the fish is just cooked, spooning water over it to poach the top. Drain on kitchen paper and cool.

2 Flake the fish into a bowl, picking out any bones or skin. Lay a piece of cling film on the surface of the fish to stop it drying out. Meanwhile, cook the potatoes in boiling salted water for 15 minutes, or until tender. Drain and return to the pan. Mash until smooth. Beat in 3 tablespoons butter and season.

3 Melt half the remaining butter in a small frying pan over a medium heat. Add the onion and cook gently for about 7 minutes, or until softened. Stir into the mashed potato mixture.

4 Beat the egg, egg yolk and chopped herbs into the potato mixture, then gently fold in the fish until well blended. Taste for seasoning and add a squeeze of lemon juice. Shape into 8 patties.

5 Put the breadcrumbs in a plastic bag. Put each fish patty into the bag in turn and shake and turn to coat completely with breadcrumbs. Arrange on a baking tray and chill for at least 20 minutes.

6 Heat about 5mm depth of oil for frying in a large, heavy-based frying pan. Add 1 tablespoon butter and heat over a medium-high heat until the butter is melted and sizzling, then swirl to blend the butter and oil. Add the fish cakes and cook for 8 minutes, or until golden brown on both sides, turning halfway through cooking. Drain on kitchen paper and serve garnished with the parsley or dill.

Menu

Crispy Fish Cakes
~
Waldorf Salad
(p.196)
~
Double-crust Apple Pie
(p.228)

Sweet Chilli Salmon

Serves 4

1 tablespoon clear honey
2 small hot red chillies, seeded and
    finely chopped
Juice of 1 lime
2 tablespoons olive oil
4 salmon steaks, about 225g each

For the salsa
3 cloves garlic, peeled
2 jalapeño chillies
3 long green chillies
1 corn cob, husks and silks removed
2 tablespoons olive oil
1 large tomato
Juice of 2 limes
2 tablespoons tequila
200g can black beans, drained
1 small red onion, finely chopped
3 tablespoons chopped fresh
    coriander
Salt and freshly ground black pepper

1 Preheat the barbecue grill to high direct heat. Mix the honey, red chillies, lime juice and 1 tablespoon oil in a bowl. Put the salmon steaks into a non-metallic dish and pour the marinade over. Cover and leave for 30 minutes.

2 Meanwhile, to make the salsa, put the garlic and jalapeños onto a metal skewer. Brush the garlic, jalapeños, long green chillies and corn with oil. Transfer the vegetables to the barbecue and cook for 8-12 minutes, or until softened and charred. Transfer the chillies to a plastic bag and leave until cool enough to handle.

3 Chop the garlic. Peel the chillies and remove the stems and seeds. Chop the flesh. Seed and chop the tomato. Remove the kernels from the corn cobs.

4 Blend the tomato, jalapeños, garlic, lime juice and tequila in a blender or food processor until fairly smooth, then transfer to a bowl. Add the remaining chopped chillies, sweetcorn kernels, black beans, red onion and coriander. Season, then cover and leave to stand until needed. Preheat the grill if cooking indoors.

5 Lift the salmon from the marinade. Transfer to the barbecue and cook over high direct heat or under the grill for 6-8 minutes, turning once and brushing occasionally with the marinade.

Menu

Sweet Chilli Salmon

~

Braised Sugar Snaps with Lettuce (p.178)

~

Baked Alaska Birthday Cake (p.235)

Tuna Noodle Casserole

Serves 6–8

90g butter or margarine
1 onion, finely chopped
2 sticks celery, thinly sliced
½ teaspoon dried thyme
4 tablespoons plain flour
Salt and freshly ground black pepper
750ml milk
125g soured cream (optional)
175g mushrooms, sliced and lightly
   sautéed in butter
175g frozen peas, thawed
225g egg noodles, cooked and drained
Two 190g cans tuna, drained
4 tablespoons dried breadcrumbs

1 Preheat the oven to 180°C/350°F/Gas mark 5. Melt 60g of the butter in a large, heavy-based saucepan over a medium heat. Add the onion, celery and thyme and cook, stirring frequently, for about 5 minutes, or until the vegetables are softened.

2 Stir in the flour and cook, stirring frequently, for about 2 minutes, or until well blended. Season with salt and pepper.

3 Gradually whisk in the milk and cook until the sauce thickens and begins to boil. Reduce the heat to low and simmer for about 10 minutes, stirring frequently. If the sauce becomes too thick, add a little more milk. Remove from the heat and stir in the soured cream.

4 Add the mushrooms, peas and noodles, and flake in the tuna. Toss well to combine and turn into a large baking dish, then spread the mixture out evenly.

5 Melt the remaining butter in a small frying pan over a medium heat. Add the breadcrumbs and stir to coat completely, then sprinkle the mixture evenly over the casserole.

6 Cook in the oven for about 25 minutes, or until the top is crisp and golden and the casserole is bubbling. Serve immediately.

Menu

Tuna Noodle Casserole

~

Sticky Toffee Pudding (p.225)

Tuna Melts

Makes about 40

20 slices white bread
5 tablespoons butter, melted
400g can tuna in oil, drained and
  flaked
115g mayonnaise
2 tablespoons chopped fresh chives
Grated zest of 2 lemons
120g Cheddar cheese, grated
Salt and freshly ground black pepper

Menu

Tuna Melts

~

*Roasted Tomato &
Goat's Cheese Salad
(p.200)*

~

*Apple Cake Bars
(p.241)*

1 Preheat the oven to 180°C/350°F/Gas mark 4. Cut out rounds of bread with a 6cm pastry cutter to make 40 croûtes – you should get 2 rounds per slice of bread. (Use the off-cuts to make breadcrumbs.)

2 Lay the bread rounds on a baking tray and brush with melted butter. Cook in the oven for 10 minutes until crisp and golden.

3 Mix the tuna with the remaining ingredients. Taste and season with salt and pepper. Place 1 heaped teaspoon of the tuna mixture on each croûte, making sure you spread the mixture to the edges of the bread so it doesn't burn when grilled. Preheat the grill.

4 Put the croûtes on a baking tray and grill for 2–3 minutes until slightly brown and just beginning to melt. Serve warm.

Grilled Tuna
with Warm Bean Salad

Serves 4

225g dried haricot beans
5 tablespoons extra virgin olive oil,
   plus extra for brushing
1 tablespoon lemon juice
1 clove garlic, finely chopped
Salt and freshly ground black pepper
1 small red onion, very finely sliced
1 tablespoon fresh parsley, chopped
4 tuna steaks, about 175g each
Fresh parsley sprigs, to garnish
Lemon wedges, to serve

Menu

*Grilled Tuna with
Warm Bean Salad*
~
*Courgette Bread
(p.208)*
~
*Stove-top
Rice Pudding with
Dried Fruit
(p.245)*

1 Cover the haricot beans in at least twice the volume of cold water and leave to soak for 8 hours or overnight.

2 When you're ready to cook, drain and rinse the beans and place in a saucepan with twice their volume of fresh water. Bring slowly to the boil, skimming off any scum that rises to the surface. Boil the beans hard for 10 minutes, then reduce the heat and simmer for a further $1\frac{1}{4}$ – $1\frac{1}{2}$ hours, or until tender.

3 Meanwhile, mix the olive oil, lemon juice, garlic and salt and pepper together in a bowl. Drain the beans thoroughly and mix together with the olive oil mixture, onion and parsley. Taste for seasoning and set aside.

4 Preheat a ridged grill pan. Wash and dry the tuna steaks. Brush lightly with oil and season. Cook on the preheated grill pan for 2 minutes on each side until just pink in the centre. Divide the bean salad among 4 serving plates. Top each with a tuna steak. Garnish each one with parsley sprigs and serve immediately with lemon wedges.

Baked Fish
with Celeriac

Serves 4

1 tablespoon olive oil
1 large onion, finely chopped
Salt and freshly ground black pepper
1 celeriac, peeled and cut into short,
  fine strips (julienne)
1kg thick white fish fillet, in 4 portions
2 tablespoons chopped fresh parsley
115g grated mature Cheddar cheese

Menu

*Baked Fish
with Celeriac*
~
*Roasted Vegetables
with Pine Nuts
& Parmesan
(p.187)*
~
*Tropical Fruit Salad
(p.221)*

1 Preheat the oven to 200°C/400°F/Gas mark 6. Heat the oil in a saucepan. Add the onion with salt and pepper, stir well, then cover and cook gently for 10 minutes. Add the celeriac, stir well and cook for a further 10 minutes, stirring occasionally.

2 Turn the celeriac and onion mixture into a shallow, ovenproof dish. Arrange the portions of fish on top and season well. Sprinkle with the parsley, then with the cheese. Cook in the oven for about 20 minutes, or until the cheese is bubbling and golden brown and the fish is just cooked. Serve at once.

Fish Finger Sandwiches

with Mayonnaise

Serves 2

8 fish fingers
Butter, for spreading
4 slices white bread
A little mayonnaise
A little tomato ketchup
Salt and freshly ground black pepper

Menu

*Fish Finger
Sandwiches with
Mayonnaise*

~

*Caesar Salad
(p.194)*

~

*Peanut Butter
Brownies
(p.240)*

Tip

Simple and super quick, this sandwich is an absolute winner for a children's party when something savoury is needed to balance out the sweets.

1 Cook the fish fingers according to the instructions on the packet. Butter the slices of bread and spread two of them with a little mayonnaise and ketchup.

2 Put the cooked fish fingers on top of the mayonnaise and ketchup, and season with a little salt and pepper. Put the remaining slices of bread on top and serve at once.

Roast Cod with Fried

Gremolata Breadcrumbs

Serves 4

2 cloves garlic, peeled

1 large bunch of fresh parsley

4 teaspoons grated lemon zest

225g breadcrumbs, made from stale ciabatta

2 tablespoons olive oil, plus extra for oiling

4 thick skinless cod fillets, about 200g each

1½ teaspoons Dijon mustard

Tip

Gremolata is a flavouring which originates from Milan, made of finely chopped lemon zest, garlic and parsley. It is usually added after a dish is cooked.

Menu

Roast Cod with Fried Gremolata Breadcrumbs

~

Aubergine Parmigiana (p.144)

1 Preheat the oven to 200°C/400°F/Gas mark 6. Put the garlic and parsley on a board and finely chop with a mezzaluna or sharp knife. Put in a bowl and stir in the lemon zest, breadcrumbs and oil.

2 Toast in a frying pan for 4-5 minutes, or until crisp and golden.

3 Put the cod fillets on an oiled baking tray. Lightly brush with the Dijon mustard and pat the breadcrumbs over the top of the fish. Cook in the oven for 10-12 minutes, or until the fish feels firm to the touch.

New England Fishballs

Makes about 25

2 tablespoons oil, plus extra for frying
1 onion, finely chopped
640g cod fillet, roughly chopped
1 tablespoon chopped fresh tarragon
1 tablespoon chopped fresh parsley
Grated zest of 1 lemon
60ml double cream
1 egg

Menu

*New England
Fishballs*
~
*Stir-fried Brown
Rice & Vegetables
(p.202)*
~
*Chocolate Fondue
with Marshmallows
(p.230)*

1 Heat the oil in a frying pan over a medium heat. Add the onion and cook for 10 minutes until softened and just golden. Set aside until cold.

2 Put the onion, cod and the remaining ingredients in a food processor and process until well mixed.

3 Shape the fish mixture into walnut-sized balls and leave to chill for 30 minutes.

4 Heat a little oil in a frying pan and cook the fishballs for 3-4 minutes each side until golden.

Smoked Trout Terrine

with Cucumber Salad

Serves 6

25g butter
25g plain flour
300ml milk
3 teaspoons fresh grated horseradish
   or good quality horseradish sauce
Salt and freshly ground black pepper
350g mayonnaise
375g cooked smoked trout fillets,
   skinned
Juice of 1 lemon
5–6 tablespoons cold water
4 sheets gelatine or 1 tablespoon
   granulated gelatine
2 egg whites

For the cucumber salad
1 cucumber, very thinly sliced
2 tablespoons white wine vinegar
1 tablespoon chopped fresh dill

1 Melt the butter in a saucepan, stir in the flour and cook for 2-3 minutes. Slowly add the milk, beating to form a smooth, thick sauce. Add the horseradish and season. Leave to cool for 15 minutes, then stir in the mayonnaise. Flake the trout into the mayonnaise mixture.

2 Mix the lemon juice with the cold water in a small saucepan and soak the gelatine for 5 minutes. Heat the gelatine until it has dissolved. Pour into the mousse mixture and mix.

3 Whisk the egg whites in a clean bowl until soft peaks form and fold into the smoked trout mixture. Spoon into a 1.2 litre terrine, which has been lined with cling film. Cover and leave to chill for 3-4 hours.

4 For the cucumber salad, place the cucumber in a shallow bowl. Pour the white wine vinegar over and stir in the dill. Season with black pepper.

5 To serve, invert the terrine on to a plate and serve in slices, along with the cucumber salad.

Menu

*Smoked Trout
Terrine with
Cucumber Salad*
~
*New England
Potato Salad
(p.172)*
~
*Double-crust
Apple Pie
(p.228)*

Harissa-coated Monkfish

Serves 4

350g couscous
350ml boiling water
2 spring onions, finely chopped
1 small bunch of fresh coriander,
   finely chopped
6 ready-to-eat dried apricots, roughly
   chopped
50g almonds, toasted and roughly
   chopped
85g raisins
1 tablespoon fresh lemon juice
4 tablespoons olive oil
Salt and freshly ground black pepper
675g monkfish tails

For the harissa
4 dried chillies
2 fresh red chillies
2 cloves garlic
2 teaspoons cumin seeds
2 teaspoons coriander seeds
2 teaspoons caraway seeds
1 tablespoon fresh lemon juice
3 tablespoons olive oil

1 Preheat the oven to 200°C/400°F/Gas mark 6. For the harissa, soak the dried chillies in boiling water for 30 minutes. Put the fresh chillies in an oven dish and roast for 20 minutes.

2 Remove the stalks from the dried and fresh chillies and put, whole, in a food processor. Add the remaining harissa ingredients and process until smooth. Spoon into a jar and chill until needed.

3 Put the couscous in a bowl and pour over the boiling water. Cover with cling film and leave to stand for 15 minutes, then fluff up with a fork.

4 Stir in the remaining ingredients, except 1 tablespoon oil and the monkfish tails, into the couscous. Season and transfer to a serving dish.

5 Cut the monkfish into 5cm medallions and put in a mixing bowl. Stir in 4 teaspoons of harissa and mix to coat every piece with the paste. Heat the remaining oil in a large frying pan and fry the fish for 2–3 minutes on each side. Arrange on top of the couscous and pour any pan juices over the top.

Menu

*Harissa-coated
Monkfish*
~
*Stir-fried Greens
with Shiitake
Mushrooms
(p.179)*
~
*Caramel Ice Cream
(p.217)*

VEGETARIAN

- Roasted Beetroot Salad with Oranges & Goat's Cheese
- Cheese & Tomato Pizza
- Chakchouka
- Cheese Fondue
- Cheese Soufflé
- Baked Macaroni & Cheese
- Eggs Benedict
- Parsley & Leek Frittata
- Spanish Omelette
- Onion Quiche
- Pasta with Fresh Tomato Sauce
- Baked Spinach Gnocchi
- Risotto Primavera
- Roast Vegetable Lasagne
- Aubergine Parmigiana
- Tomato Risotto
- Pumpkin Couscous
- Vegetable Stir-fry
- Mixed Vegetable Curry
- Black Bean Chilli with Guacamole
- Spinach with Paneer
- Chow Mein with Mangetout
- Roast Peppers with Mozzarella
- Provençal Ratatouille
- Potato Pancakes with Creamy Mushrooms
- Spinach Roulade
- Butternut Squash with Goat's Cheese

CHAPTER FOUR

VEGETARIAN

Roasted Beetroot Salad

with Oranges & Goat's Cheese

Serves 4

6 medium-sized fresh beetroots, washed

1 tablespoon balsamic vinegar

1 teaspoon honey

4 tablespoons olive oil

2 oranges

150g goat's cheese

1 tablespoon chopped fresh chives

Menu

Roasted Beetroot Salad with Oranges & Goat's Cheese

~

Grilled Corn Cobs with Flavoured Butter (p.174)

~

New England Blueberry Pancakes (p.226)

Tip

As well as the lovely rich colour it gives to soups, beetroot juice can be used to colour homemade pasta.

1 Preheat the oven to 180°C/350°F/Gas mark 4. Pierce the beetroots with a skewer or point of a knife and put in a roasting tin. Roast for 1½ hours until tender. Cool then peel off the skins. Cut into 1cm thick slices and put into a serving bowl.

2 Mix the vinegar, honey and oil together and pour over the roasted beetroots.

3 With a serrated fruit knife, peel the oranges and cut into segments. Add to the beetroots and crumble the goat's cheese on top. Scatter with chives before serving.

Cheese & Tomato Pizza

Serves 4

450g strong bread flour, plus extra
   for dusting
1 teaspoon salt
1 teaspoon dried mixed herbs
1 tablespoon fast action dried yeast
About 250–300ml hand hot water
Vegetable oil, for oiling

For the topping
800g can chopped tomatoes
4 tablespoons tomato purée
2 cloves garlic, crushed
2 teaspoons sugar
120g cheese, such as Cheddar or
   Emmental, grated
6 olives

1 Put the flour in a bowl, add the salt, herbs and yeast. Stir well. Add enough warm water to form a smooth dough. Turn on to a floured surface and knead for 10 minutes.

2 Put the dough in a large bowl that has been lightly brushed with oil. Leave in a warm place for about 1 hour, or until doubled in size.

3 For the topping, put the chopped tomatoes, tomato purée, garlic and sugar in a large frying pan and bring the mixture to the boil. Reduce the heat and simmer for 40 minutes until thickened.

4 Roll out the dough into a 33 x 26cm rectangle, and put on an oiled baking tray. Spread the tomato sauce over the dough, leaving a 5cm gap around the edge. Sprinkle over the cheese and olives, and leave to rise in a warm place for 10 minutes. Preheat the oven to 220°C/425°F/Gas mark 7.

5 Cook in the oven for 20 minutes. Cut into squares and serve warm.

Menu

*Cheese & Tomato
Pizza*
~
*Green Bean &
Mozzarella Salad
(p.201)*
~
*Roasted Corn Salsa
(p.162)*

Chakchouka

Spicy Baked Peppers

Serves 4

Menu

Chakchouka

~

Lychees with Orange & Ginger (p.229)

4 tablespoons olive oil

2 large onions, finely chopped

2 red peppers, seeded and cut into 2.5cm pieces

1 yellow pepper, seeded and cut into 2.5cm pieces

1 green pepper, seeded and cut into 2.5cm pieces

8 large tomatoes, peeled, seeded and chopped

3 cloves garlic, peeled

1 small fresh green chilli

1 teaspoon paprika

1 teaspoon ground cumin

2 teaspoons salt

1 teaspoon freshly ground black pepper

4 eggs

1 tablespoon finely chopped fresh parsley or coriander, to garnish

Steamed couscous, to serve

1 Preheat the oven to 180°C/350°F/Gas mark 4. Heat half the oil in a heavy-based frying pan. Add the onions and peppers and sauté over a high heat until the onions are soft but not brown. Add the tomatoes and simmer, uncovered, for 20–30 minutes, or until all the liquid has evaporated.

2 Using a mortar and pestle or a food processor, purée the garlic with the chilli, paprika, cumin and salt and pepper. Stir the purée into the cooked vegetables.

3 Transfer the mixture to an ovenproof dish. Smooth the surface, then make four depressions with the back of a spoon. Break an egg into each depression and sprinkle the remaining oil evenly over the top of the eggs and vegetables. Cook in the oven for 10 minutes, or until the eggs are just set. Sprinkle with parsley or coriander and serve with steaming couscous.

Cheese Fondue

Serves 4-6

Menu

Cheese Fondue
~
*Roasted Vegetables
with Pine Nuts
& Parmesan
(p.187)*

3 cloves garlic, bruised
600ml dry white wine
675g grated Gruyère or Emmental
   cheese
3 tablespoons arrowroot or plain flour
3 tablespoons butter
Salt and freshly ground white pepper
Freshly grated nutmeg
60ml whipping cream
3 tablespoons Kirsch
French bread, cut into cubes and
   lightly toasted, to serve
Boiled small new potatoes, to serve

1 Bring the garlic and white wine to the boil in a medium, heavy-based saucepan. Boil until reduced by about a quarter. Remove and discard the garlic and reduce the heat to low.

2 Toss the cheese with the arrowroot or flour in a bowl. Add half the butter to the wine and begin adding the cheese a little at a time, stirring with a wooden fork or spoon until each addition has completely melted before adding more. When all the cheese has been added, season with salt, pepper and freshly grated nutmeg to taste.

3 Add the remaining butter and half the cream and continue to cook for 2-3 minutes, until the mixture thickens to resemble thick custard in texture. Add the remaining cream and then stir in the Kirsch.

4 Pour the fondue into a warm fondue pot and set over its burner. Serve with the bread and vegetables. Provide long-handled fondue forks to spear and dunk pieces of bread or vegetable into the fondue. Using a twisting motion to remove the food from the fondue catches the delicious drips.

Cheese Soufflé

Serves 4

3 tablespoons butter, plus extra for
  greasing
25g fresh Parmesan cheese, grated
50g plain flour
300ml milk
4 eggs, separated
100g Gruyère, Emmental or
  Appenzeller, grated
2 tablespoons fresh chives, chopped
Salt and freshly ground black pepper

1 Preheat the oven to 190°C/375°F/Gas mark 5. Set the shelves in the oven so that the top shelf is in the centre of the oven with no shelves or grill pan above it. Generously grease a 3 litre soufflé dish. Sprinkle the Parmesan cheese into the dish and turn it so that the cheese sticks to the butter on the sides and bottom. Set aside.

2 Melt the butter in a medium saucepan. Add the flour and stir well until smooth. Cook gently for 1-2 minutes, then remove the pan from the heat and add about 3 tablespoons of the milk. Stir well using a wooden spoon. The mixture will appear lumpy and dry but keep stirring until smooth. Add another 3 tablespoons of the milk and stir again. Keep adding milk gradually and stirring until smooth. When half the milk is added, switch to a whisk and continue adding the milk in small amounts.

Menu

Cheese Soufflé
~
*Caesar Salad
(p.194)*
~
*Maple-baked Acorn
Squash (p.189)*

3 When all the milk is added, return the pan to a medium heat. Bring slowly up to the boil, whisking continuously, until thickened and bubbling. Reduce the heat to a gentle simmer and cook for 2 minutes, then remove. Cover and leave to cool for 5-10 minutes.

4 Add the egg yolks and whisk in thoroughly. Add the cheese and chives and stir together. Season generously - the egg white is going to dilute this mixture, so it's fine to overseason.

5 Put the egg whites into a very clean bowl and whisk until stiff peaks form. Transfer a large spoonful of egg white to the cheese mixture and fold together. Add the remaining egg white and fold together carefully, but thoroughly. Pour the mixture into the soufflé dish and transfer to the centre shelf of the oven. Cook in the oven for 25-30 minutes until well risen but firm. It should be soft, not liquid, in the middle.

Baked Macaroni & Cheese

Serves 4–6

4 tablespoons butter, plus extra
  for 'dotting'
Salt and freshly ground black
  pepper
450g macaroni
1 large onion, finely chopped
75g plain flour
1 litre milk
1 bay leaf
½ teaspoon chopped fresh thyme, plus
  extra to garnish
½ teaspoon cayenne pepper
1 teaspoon mustard powder
2 small leeks, finely chopped,
  blanched and drained
450g mature Cheddar cheese, grated
2 tablespoons dried natural
  breadcrumbs
2 tablespoons freshly grated
  Parmesan cheese

1 Preheat the oven to 180°C/350°F/Gas mark 4 and lightly grease a 33 x 23cm baking dish. Cook the macaroni in a large saucepan of boiling water for about 10 minutes, or until al dente. Drain and rinse under cold running water, then set aside.

2 Melt the butter in a heavy-based saucepan, over a medium-low heat. Add the onion and cook until translucent, stirring frequently. Sprinkle over the flour and stir until blended. Cook for 2–3 minutes.

3 Whisk in a quarter of the milk, then gradually whisk in the remaining milk. Add the bay leaf, thyme, season with salt and then simmer for about 15 minutes, or until thick and smooth. Season with the black pepper, cayenne and mustard powder.

4 Remove the sauce from the heat and stir in the drained leeks and all but a handful of the grated Cheddar. When the cheese has melted and is well blended, stir in the cooked macaroni. Transfer to the baking dish and spread out evenly. Put the dish on a large baking tray.

5 Sprinkle the remaining Cheddar over the macaroni. Combine the breadcrumbs and Parmesan, and sprinkle on top. Dot with butter and cook in the oven for 30 minutes, or until well browned and crisp. Garnish with thyme and serve.

Menu

Baked Macaroni
& Cheese
~
Waldorf Salad
(p.196)
~
Chocolate Mousse
(p.232)

Eggs Benedict

Serves 4

1 tablespoon white wine vinegar
4 extra large, very fresh eggs
2 English muffins, split, toasted and buttered
Watercress sprigs, to garnish

For the Hollandaise Sauce
3 egg yolks
2 tablespoons freshly squeezed lemon juice
½ teaspoon salt
Pinch of cayenne pepper
120g butter
2 tablespoons single cream

1 Prepare the Hollandaise sauce first. Put the egg yolks and lemon juice in a blender or food processor. Season with salt and cayenne pepper to taste and process for 15 seconds until blended.

2 Melt the butter in a small saucepan over a medium heat until bubbling and skim off any foam. With the motor running, pour the hot butter into the blender or food processor in a thin, steady stream – do not pour in the milky solids at the bottom of the pan.

3 Process for a few seconds until the sauce is well blended. Add the cream and pulse until blended. Scrape the sauce into a heatproof bowl and keep warm over hot water.

4 Bring about 2.5cm depth of water to the boil in a large frying pan. Stir in the vinegar. Break an egg into a cup. Using a wooden spoon, stir the water in a corner of the pan to create a swirl or vortex, then gently slide the egg into the middle. Repeat with the remaining eggs.

5 Reduce the heat and simmer for 3-4 minutes until the eggs are lightly cooked or set to your taste. Using a slotted spoon, transfer the eggs to a plate lined with kitchen paper to drain. Trim off any ragged edges of egg white.

6 Top each buttered muffin half with a poached egg. Spoon a little warm sauce over the eggs, garnish each with a sprig of watercress and serve.

Menu

Eggs Benedict
~
*Green Bean &
Mozzarella Salad
(p.201)*
~
*Chilled Mandarin
& Lemon Mousse
(p.233)*

Parsley & Leek Frittata

Serves 4

3 leeks
25g butter
2 small bunches of fresh parsley
4 large eggs
Salt and freshly ground black pepper

Menu

*Parsley & Leek
Frittata
~
Grapefruit, Prawn
& Avocado Salad
(p.102)*

Tip

Various fillings may be
used such as diced
mushrooms, asparagus,
spinach or cooked
diced potato.

1 Finely slice the leeks on the diagonal. Melt the butter in a medium-sized frying pan and add the leeks. Cook for 8–10 minutes until soft.

2 Preheat the grill. Remove the stalks from the parsley and finely chop with a mezzaluna. Stir into the leeks.

3 Beat the eggs and season with salt and pepper. Pour into the frying pan and cook gently for about 10 minutes. The base of the frittata should be set, but the top will be wobbly.

4 Place the frying pan under the grill and cook for 3-4 minutes until the top is set and golden.

Spanish Omelette

Serves 2

2 potatoes, peeled and thinly sliced
4 tablespoons olive oil
1 large onion, thinly sliced
2 eggs
Salt and freshly ground black pepper
Crusty bread, to serve

Menu

Spanish Omelette
~
Panzanella
(p.198)
~
Spiced Baked Apples
(p.224)

1 Heat the oil in a frying pan. Add the potato and onion and cook very gently until tender, without browning if possible.

2 While the potato and onion are cooking, beat the eggs with some seasoning in a large bowl.

3 Lift the potato and onion from the pan using a slotted spoon and add to the eggs. Drain all but about 1 tablespoon of the oil from the pan. Return the egg mixture to the pan, shaking it to distribute everything evenly. Cook gently until the egg is set and lightly golden on the bottom.

4 Put a plate that is larger than the pan over the top and carefully invert the omelette on to it. Slide the omelette back into the pan, cooked-side-uppermost, and continue to cook until the bottom is set and golden. This omelette can be served hot, warm or cold.

Onion Quiche

Serves 6

115g butter
225g plain flour, plus extra for dusting
2 tablespoons cold water

For the filling
2 tablespoons butter
450g onions, thinly sliced
3 eggs, beaten
300ml single cream
3 tablespoons dry sherry
Pinch of ground mace
Salt and freshly ground black pepper

1 To make the dough, rub the butter into the flour until the mixture resembles fine breadcrumbs. Stir in the cold water to form a dough, then knead lightly. Wrap in cling film and chill 30 minutes.

2 Roll out the dough on a lightly floured surface and use to line a 25cm loose-bottom tart tin or quiche dish. Prick the base all over and chill for a further 30 minutes.

3 Preheat the oven to 200°C/400°F/Gas mark 6. Line the pastry case with greaseproof paper and weigh down with baking beans or dried beans. Bake for 10 minutes, then remove the beans and paper. Reduce the oven temperature to 180°C/350°F/ Gas mark 4.

4 Meanwhile, make the filling. Melt the butter in a heavy-based saucepan and add the onions. Stir well, then cook for 10 minutes, or until softened but not browned. Remove from the heat and cool slightly.

5 Beat the eggs with the cream, sherry, mace and plenty of seasoning. Use a slotted spoon to transfer the cooked onions to the pastry case, distributing them evenly over the base, and pour any cooking juices into the egg mixture. Stir well, then pour the mixture over the onions. Bake the quiche for about 45 minutes, or until the filling is set and golden brown. Leave to cool for 15 minutes before serving. The quiche can be enjoyed warm or cold.

Menu

Onion Quiche
~
*Roasted Vegetables
with Pine Nuts
& Parmesan
(p.187)*
~
*Meringues with
Cream & Blueberries
(p.223)*

Pasta with Fresh

Tomato Sauce

Serves 2

1kg ripe plum or beef tomatoes
3 tablespoons olive oil
1 small onion, finely chopped
1 clove garlic, crushed
2 tablespoons fresh basil, chopped
Pinch of sugar
Salt and freshly ground black pepper
115g dried pasta of your choice
Freshly grated Parmesan cheese, to
   serve
Green salad, to serve

1 Put the tomatoes into a large bowl and pour boiling water over to cover. Leave for 30 seconds, then drain and refresh under cold water. Using a sharp knife, prick the skin of each tomato – it should split and come away easily from the tomato. If not, you may have to repeat the process for a further 30 seconds. Skin the tomatoes and chop. Set aside.

Menu

*Pasta with Fresh
Tomato Sauce*
~
*Old-fashioned
Cornbread
(p.210)*

2 Heat the oil in a large saucepan. Add the onion and cook over a medium heat for about 5 minutes, stirring frequently, until softened but not browned. Add the garlic and cook for a further 30 seconds. Add the tomatoes, basil and sugar and stir well. Bring to the boil and cover. Simmer for 45 minutes. Remove the lid and simmer, uncovered, for 45-60 minutes until thickened. Taste and adjust the seasoning.

3 Cook the pasta according to the instructions on the packet and serve immediately with the fresh tomato sauce, sprinkled with Parmesan cheese, and a green salad on the side. Alternatively, this sauce can be frozen for up to 3 months.

Baked Spinach Gnocchi

Serves 4

3 tablespoons extra virgin olive oil
2 spring onions, chopped
1 clove garlic, crushed
225g fresh spinach
475ml milk
100g semolina
Freshly grated nutmeg
1 egg, beaten
75g freshly grated Parmesan cheese
Salt and freshly ground black pepper

1 Heat the olive oil, spring onions and garlic in a large saucepan. When the onions begin to sizzle, add the spinach and stir well. Cover and cook for 30 seconds. Stir, then remove from the heat.

2 Cool the spinach slightly, then transfer the mixture to a blender and finely chop. If you do not have a blender, drain bundles of the mixture, reserving all the liquid, and chop them by hand, then return them to the reserved juices.

3 Pour the milk into the pan used to cook the spinach and heat until boiling. Sprinkle in the semolina, stirring all the time. Cook until boiling, first stirring, then beating as it thickens. After 1 minute, the semolina should be thick and come away from the sides of the pan. Remove from the heat and stir in the spinach mixture. Season and add nutmeg to taste. Leave to cool slightly, then beat in the egg.

4 Lightly oil a shallow dish. Turn the semolina mixture out on to it, spreading the mixture to a rectangle of about 18 x 25cm. Pat the edges with a knife then cover with cling film, and chill for at least 2 hours.

5 Preheat the oven to 200°C/400°F/Gas mark 6 and lightly oil a 25cm round ovenproof dish. Cut the semolina into 3 strips slightly more than 5cm wide. Wet the knife, then wipe with kitchen paper; wet it again between cuts. Cut the mixture at 25cm intervals in the opposite direction to give 15 gnocchi.

6 Dip each square in grated Parmesan to coat both sides, and place in the dish. Overlap the squares around the edge of the dish, then place a few in the middle to fill. Sprinkle with remaining Parmesan and bake in the oven for 30 minutes until crisp and golden on top. Serve immediately.

Menu

Baked Spinach Gnocchi

~

Hot Vegetable Salad (p.184)

~

Apple Cake Bars (p.241)

Risotto Primavera

Serves 6

2 tablespoons butter
1 tablespoon olive oil
1 onion, finely chopped
1 stick celery, finely chopped
2 carrots, peeled and finely chopped
375g arborio rice
750ml vegetable stock
55g fresh peas
2 medium courgettes, finely chopped
Salt and freshly ground black pepper
Small bunch of fresh mint, finely
  chopped
Small bunch of fresh parsley, finely
  chopped
Shavings of Parmesan cheese, to serve

1 Melt the butter with the oil in a large heavy-based saucepan and add the vegetables. Cover and cook for 15 minutes.

2 Add the rice to the pan and stir well to coat the grains of rice. Pour in 120ml stock and stir. Cook until the liquid has been absorbed.

3 Add the same amount of stock and the peas, stir a few times and again leave to let the rice absorb the liquid. Continue in this way for 25 minutes leaving 120ml stock aside.

4 Stir the courgettes into the risotto with the remaining stock. Stir well and season with salt and pepper.

5 Mix the fresh herbs into the risotto and serve immediately with shavings of Parmesan.

Menu

Risotto Primavera
~
*Caesar Salad
(p.194)*
~
*Summer Berry
Shortcakes
(p.246)*

Roast Vegetable Lasagne

Serves 4

1 large red pepper, seeded and cut into chunks

2 small courgettes, cut into chunks

2 red onions, each cut into 8 wedges

4 cloves garlic

1 medium aubergine, cut into chunks

2 tablespoons olive oil

2 large fresh thyme sprigs

2 fresh bay leaves

Two 300g jars fresh tomato sauce

275g jar artichokes in oil, drained and halved if large

55g sun-dried tomatoes

4 tablespoons freshly grated Parmesan

500g ricotta cheese

2 eggs, beaten

Salt and freshly ground black pepper

About 9 fresh lasagne sheets

1 Preheat the oven to 200°C/400°F/Gas mark 6. Toss the pepper, courgettes, onions, whole garlic cloves and aubergine with the oil in a large bowl. Tip everything on to a shallow roasting tray or heavy-based baking tray. Tuck the thyme sprigs and bay leaves among the vegetables. Cook near the top of the oven, turning twice, for about 40 minutes until tender and golden at the edges. Reduce the oven temperature to 190°C/375°F/Gas mark 5.

2 Remove the whole herbs. Mix the vegetables with the tomato sauce, artichokes and sun-dried tomatoes. Set aside.

3 Reserve about 3 tablespoons of the Parmesan cheese, then, in a large bowl, beat the ricotta until soft, then mix in the eggs, remaining Parmesan cheese and plenty of seasoning. Set aside.

4 Spread a large spoonful of the vegetable mixture over the bottom of an ovenproof dish measuring about 20 x 25 x 6cm. Trimming the sheets to fit, top with a layer of pasta. Now add half the remaining vegetable mixture and top with half the remaining pasta. Add the last of the vegetable mixture and the final layer of pasta and top with the ricotta mixture. Sprinkle with the reserved Parmesan cheese.

5 Bake in the centre of the oven for about 40-45 minutes, or until bubbling and golden.

Menu

Roast Vegetable Lasagne
~
Panzanella
(p.198)
~
Caramel Ice Cream
(p.217)

Aubergine Parmigiana

Serves 6

Olive oil, for oiling and frying
2 eggs, beaten with 1 tablespoon water
65g natural dried breadcrumbs
1 large aubergine, cut into 1cm slices
45g freshly grated Parmesan cheese
225g mozzarella cheese, thinly sliced

For the tomato sauce
2 tablespoons olive oil
1 large onion, finely chopped
2–3 cloves garlic, finely chopped
Two 400g cans chopped tomatoes
2 teaspoons brown sugar
1 bay leaf
1 teaspoon dried oregano
1 teaspoon dried basil
Salt and freshly ground black pepper
2 tablespoons shredded fresh basil

Menu

Aubergine
Parmigiana
~
Texas Pilaf
(p.203)

1 For the tomato sauce, heat the oil in a heavy-based saucepan. Cook the onion for 7 minutes, or until it is soft and translucent, stirring occasionally. Add the garlic and cook for another minute, then add the tomatoes, sugar, bay leaf, oregano and dried basil, and bring to the boil, stirring frequently. Reduce the heat and simmer, stirring occasionally, for 30-45 minutes, or until the sauce has thickened. Season, stir in the basil and remove from the heat.

2 Lightly oil a large, shallow baking dish and set aside. Put the beaten egg in a shallow dish and the breadcrumbs on a sheet of greaseproof paper. Dip slices of aubergine into the egg mixture and then into the breadcrumbs to coat each side completely.

3 Heat 2-3 tablespoons oil in a heavy-based frying pan. Cook a few aubergine slices at a time, turning regularly, until golden. Add more oil if needed. Drain on kitchen paper. Repeat with all the slices.

4 Preheat the oven to 180°C/350°F/Gas mark 4. Spread a little tomato sauce in the dish. Arrange a layer of aubergine slices over the sauce, sprinkle with Parmesan and top with a layer of mozzarella slices, then cover with a layer of sauce. Repeat the layers, ending with a thin layer of tomato sauce and a sprinkle of Parmesan. Drizzle a little oil on top and bake for 35 minutes, or until bubbling and brown.

Tomato Risotto

Serves 4

500g tomatoes, skinned and halved
60ml extra virgin olive oil
1 large onion, finely chopped
1 clove garlic, crushed
270g arborio or risotto rice
240ml dry white wine
600ml vegetable stock
Salt and freshly ground black pepper
1 teaspoon sugar

Menu

Tomato Risotto
~
Braised Fennel
(p.177)
~
Mango Ice Cream
(p.216)

1 Scoop the seeds and any soft pulp out of the tomatoes into a sieve. Press the pulp through the sieve and discard the seeds. Finely dice the tomato shells and set both these and the sieved pulp aside.

2 Heat the olive oil in a large saucepan. Add the onion and garlic and cook, stirring occasionally, for about 5 minutes, or until the onion has softened slightly. Add the rice and stir until all the grains are coated in oil. Pour in the wine and the sieved tomato pulp, then bring to the boil. Reduce the heat and simmer, uncovered, stirring once or twice, until the liquid is virtually absorbed.

3 Meanwhile, heat the stock to simmering point in a separate saucepan. Keeping it just below simmering point, add about a quarter of the stock to the risotto with seasoning to taste. Stir well and simmer until all the stock has been absorbed. Add the remaining stock in 3 batches, simmering until each batch is absorbed before adding the next. Stir in the diced tomatoes and sugar with the final batch of stock.

4 Remove the risotto from the heat and cover the pan tightly, then leave to stand for 5 minutes. Fork up the rice and season, then serve at once.

Pumpkin Couscous

Serves 4

3 tablespoons olive oil
2 cloves garlic, crushed
2 onions, finely chopped
1 green pepper, seeded and chopped
1 yellow pepper, seeded and chopped
1 tablespoon dried sage
900g prepared pumpkin, cut into 1cm
   cubes
Two 400g cans chopped tomatoes
400g can chickpeas, drained
Salt and freshly ground black pepper
260g couscous
400ml boiling water
1 large mild green chilli, such as
   Anaheim, seeded and chopped
1 hot chilli, such as jalapeño or
   serrano, seeded and chopped
Grated zest of 1 lemon
3 tablespoons chopped fresh parsley,
   plus extra to garnish
A little extra virgin olive oil (optional)

1 Heat the olive oil in a saucepan. Add the garlic, onions and green and yellow peppers. Stir well, then cover the pan and cook over a medium heat for 15 minutes until the vegetables have softened.

2 Stir in the sage and pumpkin, then pour in the tomatoes with their juice. Mix in the chickpeas and season with salt and pepper. Bring to the boil, reduce the heat and cover. Simmer for 25-30 minutes.

3 When the pumpkin has been cooking for 5-10 minutes, place the couscous in a heatproof bowl. Sprinkle with a little salt. Pour in the boiling water, cover and leave to stand for 15 minutes. In a separate bowl, mix the mild and hot chillies with the lemon zest and parsley.

4 Taste the pumpkin and season if necessary. Add the chilli, lemon and parsley mixture and remove from the heat. Stir lightly. Fluff the couscous with a fork and drizzle with a little extra virgin olive oil, if using, then season with freshly ground black pepper. Divide the couscous among 4 large warm bowls. Ladle the pumpkin casserole over the couscous, garnish with parsley, and serve at once.

Menu

*Pumpkin
Couscous*
~
*Green Bean &
Mozzarella Salad
(p.201)*
~
*Old-fashioned
Cornbread (p.210)*

Vegetable Stir-fry

Serves 4

350g mixed prepared vegetables, such
    as baby corn, red pepper, pak choi,
    mushrooms, broccoli, carrot
2 tablespoons light soy sauce
1 tablespoon rice wine or dry sherry
2 tablespoons vegetable stock or water
2 tablespoons groundnut oil
350g tofu, cubed
2 cloves garlic, finely chopped
2.5cm piece fresh root ginger, chopped
3 spring onions, finely chopped
1 red chilli, seeded and finely chopped
1 teaspoon cornflour
1 teaspoon water
1 teaspoon sesame oil
Toasted cashews, shredded spring
    onions and bean sprouts, to garnish

1 Halve the baby corn lengthways, seed and thinly
slice the red pepper, tear or shred the pak choi,
slice the mushrooms, break the broccoli into florets
and slice the carrot into batons. Mix the soy sauce,
rice wine and stock together, then set aside.

2 Put the wok over a high heat until it is very
hot. Add the groundnut oil and swirl it to lightly
coat the wok. Leave for a few seconds until the oil
is almost smoking – a fine haze will appear.

3 Add the tofu and move it around the wok continuously for 1-2 minutes, or until it starts to brown.

4 Add the garlic, ginger, spring onions and chilli. Cook for a few seconds, continuing to stir.

5 Add the prepared vegetables in the following order: carrot, broccoli, pepper and mushrooms. Cook for about 1 minute before adding the baby corn and pak choi. Cook for another minute, still stirring and turning everything over a high heat.

6 Add the soy sauce mixture to the wok. Mix the cornflour with the water until smooth. Add to the wok and stir. Bring to the boil, reduce the heat and simmer for 1 minute until thickened and everything is coated in sauce. Remove from the heat.

7 Add the sesame oil and mix together well. Transfer the stir-fry to serving bowls and scatter over the toasted cashews, shredded spring onions and bean sprouts.

Menu

Vegetable Stir-fry
~
Coconut Rice
(p.206)

Mixed Vegetable Curry

Serves 6

90g butter or vegetable oil

1 large onion, finely chopped

2 cloves garlic, crushed

2.5cm fresh root ginger, peeled and finely chopped

1 teaspoon dark mustard seeds

Seeds of 4 green cardamom pods

1 teaspoon ground cumin

1 teaspoon ground coriander

1 teaspoon ground turmeric

2 potatoes, cut into bite-sized pieces

2 carrots, cut into bite-sized sticks

2 green or red peppers, halved and cut into thick slices

115g green beans, cut into thirds on the diagonal

2 aubergines, cut into 2.5cm cubes

2 small courgettes, sliced

400ml can unsweetened coconut milk

1 teaspoon sugar

3 tablespoons chopped fresh coriander

3 tablespoons chopped fresh mint

2 teaspoons salt

2 chopped fresh green chillies and/or 2 tablespoons unsweetened shredded coconut, to garnish

1 Heat the butter or oil in a heavy-based saucepan or casserole. Add the onion, garlic, ginger and mustard seeds and sauté over a high heat for 2 minutes. Add the cardamom seeds, cumin, coriander and turmeric and cook for 1 minute.

2 Add the potatoes, coating well with the spice mixture. One at a time, add the carrots, peppers, green beans, aubergines and courgettes, coating each with the spice mixture as before.

3 Add the coconut milk and sugar. Bring to the boil and add the coriander, mint and salt. Reduce the heat and simmer for about 20 minutes, or until the vegetables are cooked. (Be careful not to overcook.)

4 Transfer to a serving dish and garnish with chillies and/or the coconut.

Menu

Mixed Vegetable Curry

~

Lychees with Orange & Ginger (p.229)

Chilli with Guacamole

Serves 6

225g dried black turtle beans or black
kidney beans
3 tablespoons olive oil
2 onions, chopped
2 cloves garlic, crushed
1 or 2 hot green chillies, seeded and
finely chopped, to taste
2 tablespoons mild chilli powder
1 teaspoon ground cumin
1 teaspoon paprika
Two 400g cans chopped tomatoes
1 teaspoon dried oregano
Salt and freshly ground black pepper
Soured cream, to serve

For the guacamole
2 medium ripe avocados, peeled and
finely chopped
1 small red onion, finely chopped
1 small red chilli, seeded and finely
chopped
2 small tomatoes, skinned, seeded and
diced
Juice of 1 lime
2 tablespoons fresh coriander,
chopped

1 Put the beans into a large bowl and cover with at least twice their volume of cold water. Leave to soak for 8 hours or overnight. Drain the beans and put into a large saucepan. Cover with fresh water and bring to the boil. Boil for 10 minutes, then reduce the heat and simmer for about 40 minutes until the beans are tender. Drain and set aside.

2 Heat the oil in a large saucepan. Add the onions and fry for 7–8 minutes until softened. Add the garlic and chillies and cook for 1 minute. Add the chilli powder, cumin and paprika and cook for 30 seconds before adding the tomatoes and oregano. Simmer gently, uncovered, for 20 minutes. Add the beans, stir well and simmer for a further 30–40 minutes until the chilli has thickened. Season.

3 To make the guacamole, put the avocados into a non-reactive copper bowl. Add the onion, chilli, tomatoes, lime juice and coriander and mix well. Serve the chilli in bowls with a spoonful of guacamole and soured cream on the side.

Menu

Black Bean Chilli with Guacamole

…

Old-fashioned Cornbread (p.210)

…

Tomato Salsa (p.162)

Spinach with Paneer

Serves 4

2 tablespoons butter or ghee
225g paneer, in one piece
1 large onion, chopped
1 clove garlic, crushed
1 tablespoon cumin seeds
1 teaspoon ground turmeric
Salt and freshly ground black pepper
1kg young spinach, coarsely shredded

Tip

Young tender spinach leaves are ideal raw in salads, and are an excellent source of vitamins A and C.

1 Melt the butter or ghee in a heavy-based saucepan. Add the paneer and cook until it is golden brown underneath, then use a spatula to turn it, and cook the other side. Remove from the pan, drain carefully and transfer to a plate.

2 Add the onion, garlic and cumin seeds to the pan. Stir well, then cook over a medium heat for about 15 minutes until the onion has thoroughly softened and is beginning to brown in places. Stir frequently and keep the heat fairly low.

3 Stir in the turmeric with plenty of salt and pepper. Add the spinach to the pan and cover tightly. Cook for 2 minutes, or until the spinach has wilted. Meanwhile, cut the paneer into small cubes.

4 Stir the spinach with the onion and cooking juices. Taste and adjust the seasoning. Top with the paneer and cook for 2 minutes to heat the cheese slightly.

Menu

Spinach
with Paneer

~

Emmental & Roasted
Corn Spoon Bread
(p.207)

~

Tropical
Fruit Salad
(p.221)

Chow Mein
with Mangetout

Serves 4

6 large dried shiitake mushrooms
350g dried Chinese egg noodles
2 teaspoons cornflour
6 tablespoons dry sherry
2 tablespoons light soy sauce
2 teaspoons sesame oil
2 tablespoons safflower oil
2 tablespoons chopped fresh
   root ginger
2 cloves garlic, crushed
225g mangetout, sliced
8 spring onions, finely chopped

1 Put the mushrooms in a small bowl and pour in just enough boiling water to cover them. Leave to soak for 10 minutes, pressing the mushrooms into the water frequently so that they rehydrate. Drain and slice the mushrooms, reserving the soaking water and discarding any tough stems.

2 Put the dried egg noodles in a large bowl, breaking the sheets in half so that they fit easily and cover with plenty of boiling water. Cover and leave to soak for 10 minutes, or until tender. Blend the cornflour to a smooth paste with the sherry, soy sauce and sesame oil. Prepare a colander or sieve for draining the noodles before beginning to stir-fry the vegetables.

Menu

Chow Mein
with Mangetout
~
Braised Sugar
Snaps with Lettuce
(p.178)
~
Lychees with
Orange & Ginger
(p.229)

3 Heat the safflower oil in a wok or large frying pan. Add the ginger and stir-fry for 30 seconds, then add the garlic, and stir-fry for another 30 seconds. Add the mushrooms and cook briefly, then add the mangetout and spring onions. Stir-fry 1 minute. Pour in the cornflour mixture and bring to the boil, stirring until thickened.

4 Drain the noodles and add them to the vegetables. Toss all the ingredients together so they are thoroughly combined. Taste for seasoning and add more soy sauce to taste if necessary. Serve immediately.

Roast Peppers
with Mozzarella

Serves 4

4 medium red peppers
16 ripe cherry tomatoes, skinned
4 fat cloves garlic, finely chopped
8 anchovy fillets, drained and finely
  chopped (optional)
Handful of fresh basil leaves, torn, plus
  extra, to garnish
8 tablespoons extra virgin olive oil
Freshly ground black pepper, to taste
150g ball mozzarella in whey, drained
  and chopped into 8 equal pieces
Crusty bread, to serve

Menu

Roast Peppers with
Mozzarella

~

Broccoli Pilaf
(p.205)

~

Chocolate-covered
Doughnuts
(p.238)

1 Preheat the oven to 200°C/400°F/ Gas mark 6.
Cut each pepper in half lengthways through the
stem. Scoop out the seeds and membranes. Put the
pepper halves on to a large baking tray.

2 Put two cherry tomatoes into each pepper
half. Divide the garlic, anchovies (if using) and
basil among the pepper halves. Drizzle each with
1 tablespoon of olive oil. Season with black pepper
(the anchovies and cheese will add enough salt).
Transfer the baking tray to the oven and cook for
40 minutes until softened and starting to brown at
the edges. Remove the tray from the oven and
divide the cheese among the peppers. Return to
the oven for a further 10 minutes, or until the
cheese is melted. Serve hot or warm with plenty
of crusty bread.

Provençal Ratatouille

Serves 4

2 bulbs fennel, quartered lengthways
3 red onions, quartered
6 cloves garlic, unpeeled
6 tablespoons olive oil
Salt and freshly ground black pepper
3 courgettes, chopped into 1cm slices
2 red peppers, seeded and cut into 5cm
  chunks
1 aubergine, cut into 5cm chunks

For the tomato sauce
400g can chopped tomatoes
150ml white wine
2 tablespoons tomato purée
6 fresh thyme sprigs
1 teaspoon sugar

Menu

Provençal Ratatouille
~
*Patatas Bravas
(p.167)*
~
*Applesauce Sundae
(p.236)*

1 Preheat the oven to 200°C/400°F/Gas mark 6. Use 2 large roasting tins. Don't try to cram all the vegetables into one or they'll end up soggy and stewed instead of roasted. Blanch the fennel in boiling water for 5 minutes, then drain. Place the onions and fennel in a roasting tin with 3 unpeeled garlic cloves and half the oil. Season well with salt and pepper.

2 Put the courgettes, peppers and aubergine into the second roasting tin. Pour the remaining oil over the vegetables and add the rest of the garlic cloves. Roast the fennel, onion and garlic in the oven for 50 minutes, and the courgettes, peppers, aubergine and garlic for 40 minutes.

3 Meanwhile, to make the tomato sauce, put the tomatoes in a saucepan and stir in the remaining ingredients. Simmer for 20 minutes until reduced and thickened. Remove the thyme sprigs and stir in the roasted vegetables.

Potato Pancakes

with Creamy Mushrooms

Serves 4 as a main course or 6 as a starter

500g cooked floury potatoes
Salt and freshly ground black pepper
3 eggs, separated
25g butter
50g plain flour
5 tablespoons milk
2 tablespoons olive oil, plus extra for frying
200g halved button or chestnut mushrooms
150ml crème fraîche or soured cream
1 tablespoon creamed horseradish
2 tablespoons chopped fresh chives

Menu

Potato Pancakes with Creamy Mushrooms
~
Bream with Garlic & Coriander Butter (p.106)
~
Tropical Fruit Salad (p.221)

1 Mash and season the potatoes. Whisk in the egg yolks, butter, flour and milk to give a soft mash.

2 Whisk the egg whites in a clean bowl until stiff peaks form, then fold into the mash.

3 Heat a little oil in a large frying pan and add large spoonfuls of the batter. Cook for 2 minutes on each side until browned, crisp and slightly souffléd. Keep warm until ready to serve.

4 Heat the 2 tablespoons of oil in a large frying pan. Add the mushrooms and cook over a high heat until browned and softened. Add the crème fraîche or soured cream and the creamed horseradish. Stir in the chives, season to taste and serve with the potato pancakes.

Spinach Roulade

Serves 4

175g fresh spinach
3 tablespoons butter, plus extra for greasing
3 tablespoons plain flour, plus extra for dusting
400ml milk
3 eggs, separated
Salt and freshly ground black pepper
¼ teaspoon freshly grated nutmeg
4 tablespoons freshly grated Parmesan cheese
200g garlic and herb cream cheese
75g ricotta cheese
2 tablespoons soured cream
2 tablespoons chopped fresh chives

Menu

Spinach
Roulade
~
Carrots with Maple
Syrup
(p.182)
~
Spiced Grilled Sweet
Potatoes (p.170)

1 Preheat the oven to 200°C/400°F/Gas mark 6. Wash the spinach and cook in a covered saucepan for 2–3 minutes until just wilted. Cool slightly, squeeze out all the moisture and finely chop. Grease and line a 23 x 33cm Swiss roll tin with greaseproof paper. Grease the paper and dust lightly with flour.

2 Melt the butter in a saucepan and stir in the flour. Cook for 1 minute, then remove from the heat. Gradually whisk in the milk, then return to the heat, and continue whisking gently until the mixture boils and thickens. Boil for 1 minute, then remove from the heat once more.

3 Whisk in the egg yolks one at a time until the mixture is smooth. Beat in the spinach, salt, pepper and nutmeg.

4 Whisk the egg whites in a clean bowl until stiff peaks form and fold into the mixture. Pour the mixture into the tin and spread out evenly. Bake for about 12–14 minutes, or until lightly set.

5 Sprinkle the Parmesan cheese over a sheet of greaseproof paper and turn the roulade out on to it. Remove the lining paper and leave to cool slightly. Beat the garlic and herb cheese, ricotta, soured cream and chives together. Spread the mixture over the roulade, then use the paper to roll it up from one long side.

Butternut Squash
with Goat's Cheese

Serves 2

1 butternut squash, about 900g in
   weight, halved and seeded
Extra virgin olive oil
Salt and freshly ground black pepper
2 spring onions, finely chopped
15g chopped fresh parsley
115g round mild goat's cheese, sliced
   horizontally in half
Green salad, to serve

Menu

*Butternut Squash
with Goat's Cheese
~
Berry Ice Lollies
(p.214)*

1 Preheat the oven to 200°C/400°F/Gas mark 6.
Cut two pieces of foil, each large enough to
enclose half of the butternut squash. Place the
squash halves on the pieces of foil and brush their
cut tops generously with olive oil. Sprinkle with salt
and pepper, then wrap the foil tightly around the
squash to enclose the halves completely. Place on a
baking tray or in an ovenproof dish and bake for
1 hour, or until the squash is completely tender.

2 Remove the squash from the oven and increase
the temperature to 220°C/425°F/Gas mark 7.
Open the foil and fold it back neatly around the
outside of the squash halves. Divide the spring
onions and parsley between the hollows in the
squash halves, and place a slice of goat's cheese
on top of each.

3 Bake the squash for a further 5-7 minutes,
or until the cheese melts and is beginning to
brown slightly around the edge. Serve at once with
a green salad.

SALADS & SIDE DISHES

- Roasted Corn Salsa
- Tomato Salsa
- Warm Cheese & Smoked Chilli Dip with Tortilla Chips
- Old-fashioned English Chips
- Luxury Mashed Potatoes
- Duchesse Potatoes
- Patatas Bravas
- Leek & Potato Layer
- Spiced Grilled Sweet Potatoes
- Latkes
- New England Potato Salad
- Succotash
- Grilled Corn Cobs with Flavoured Butter
- Sweet Potato Casserole with Marshmallow Topping
- Braised Fennel

- Braised Sugar Snaps with Lettuce
- Stir-Fried Greens with Shiitake Mushrooms
- Broad Beans with Prosciutto
- Potato & Beetroot Mash
- Carrots with Maple Syrup
- Brussels Sprouts with Sweet Potatoes
- Hot Vegetable Salad
- Spiced Courgettes
- Roasted Vegetables with Pine Nuts & Parmesan
- Cauliflower & Leek Patties
- Maple-baked Acorn Squash
- Mexican Pot Beans
- Classic Healthy Coleslaw
- Spinach & Mushroom Salad with Hot Bacon Dressing

- Caesar Salad
- Chickpea & Tomato Salad
- Waldorf Salad
- Chef's Salad
- Panzanella
- Roasted Tomato & Goat's Cheese Salad
- Green Bean & Mozzarella Salad
- Stir-fried Brown Rice & Vegetables
- Texas Pilaf
- Broccoli Pilaf
- Coconut Rice
- Egg-fried Rice
- Emmental & Roasted Corn Spoon Bread
- Courgette Bread
- Old-fashioned Cornbread
- Bacon & Caramelized Onion Rolls

CHAPTER FIVE

SALADS & SIDE DISHES

Roasted Corn Salsa

Serves 4

3 corn cobs
600g tomatoes, skinned, seeded
   and diced
1 red chilli, seeded and finely chopped
1 green chilli, seeded and
   finely chopped
3 tablespoons olive oil
1 tablespoon chopped fresh parsley
Salt and freshly ground black pepper

1 Preheat a grill or stovetop grill pan. Put the corn cobs under the grill or in the grill pan and cook for about 10 minutes, turning them frequently.

2 Leave to cool, then with a sharp knife remove the kernels. Put the kernels in a bowl. Add the tomatoes, chillies, oil and parsley and season well with salt and pepper. Mix together and serve.

Tomato Salsa

Serves 4–6

8 plum tomatoes, skinned and chopped
2 tablespoons tomato purée
2 green chillies, such as jalapeño or
   serrano, seeded and chopped
4 spring onions, chopped
4 cloves garlic, finely chopped
15g chopped fresh coriander
Grated zest and juice of 1 lime
Salt and freshly ground black pepper
2 teaspoons sugar
60ml extra virgin olive oil

1 Mix the tomatoes and tomato purée in a bowl until thoroughly combined. Stir in the chillies, onions, garlic, coriander, lime zest and juice, sugar and plenty of salt and pepper. Stir until the sugar and salt have dissolved, then stir in the olive oil.

2 Cover the salsa with cling film or decant into a plastic storage container and leave to marinate in the refrigerator for at least 4 hours before serving. If possible, make it a day in advance and chill overnight. This is best served lightly chilled.

Warm Cheese & Smoked
Chilli Dip with Tortilla Chips

Serves 4

Vegetable oil, for deep-frying
4 soft wheat tortillas, cut into triangles

For the dip
1 tablespoon butter
5 spring onions, finely chopped
1 chipotle (smoked) chilli, soaked
   in hot water for 20 minutes
300ml double cream
300g Cheddar cheese, grated

1 Heat the oil in a large deep saucepan to 190°C/375°F and cook the tortillas for 2-3 minutes. Drain on kitchen paper.

2 Melt the butter in another saucepan. Add the spring onions and cook for 5 minutes.

3 Drain the chipotle chilli and finely chop. Stir the chilli into the onions, then add the cream and cheese. Cook over a low heat until the cheese has melted. Serve warm with the tortilla chips to dip.

Tip
A tortilla is a round, flat unleavened pancake often called 'bread of Mexico'. Cut into triangles, tortillas serve as spoons for dipping.

Old-fashioned
English Chips

Serves 4

6 medium-sized Russet potatoes, peeled
Vegetable oil, for deep frying

For the mayonnaise
1 whole egg
2 egg yolks
2 teaspoons English mustard powder
1 tablespoon white wine vinegar
300ml light olive oil or groundnut oil
1 tablespoon fresh lemon juice
   (optional)

Tip
To deep-fat fry safely, you should only fill the pan one-third full. Never fry wet potatoes and never leave the pan unattended.

1 Peel the potatoes with a small knife or a vegetable peeler, then using a large chef's knife, cut off the rounded edges to make the potatoes into even rectangles. Cut each potato rectangle into 1cm wide strips, then again lengthways into chips. Fill a bowl with cold water and drop in the chips as they are made. This removes the starch. Set aside while the oil heats up.

2 Heat the vegetable oil for deep-frying in a deep fat fryer or large saucepan to 170°C/325°F. Drain the potatoes well and pat dry on kitchen paper. Deep-fry in batches for 6–8 minutes, or until soft and pale, transferring to a plate lined with kitchen paper.

3 Increase the temperature of the oil to 190°C/375°F. Re-fry the chips, in batches, for 3–4 minutes until crisp and golden. Drain on kitchen paper and keep warm.

4 For the mayonnaise, put the egg and egg yolks in a food processor with the mustard and vinegar and process for a few seconds. With the motor running, slowly pour in the olive oil. If it is very thick, blend in the lemon juice. Serve with the chips.

Luxury Mashed Potatoes

Serves 4–6

1kg potatoes, peeled and halved
Salt and freshly ground white pepper
300ml single cream
50g butter

1 Put the potatoes in a saucepan and pour in just enough boiling water to cover them. Add a little salt, bring to the boil and reduce the heat. Cover the pan and simmer for 15 minutes. Drain well.

2 Return the potatoes to the pan and pour in the cream. Replace the pan on the heat and stir well. Bring to the boil, then simmer for 5 minutes, stirring frequently, until the potatoes are breaking up. Add the butter and plenty of white pepper, then mash until smooth. Remove from the heat, taste for seasoning and serve at once.

Duchesse Potatoes

Serves 4

1.2kg maincrop potatoes, peeled
Salt
55g butter, plus extra for brushing
125ml milk
2 egg yolks

1 Halve the potatoes and cook them in a large saucepan of boiling salted water until tender, then drain well and mash. Heat the butter and milk in another saucepan and pour the mixture over the potatoes. Beat for a couple of minutes with a hand-held electric mixer. Leave to cool, then mix in the egg yolks.

2 Preheat the oven to 200°C/400°F/Gas mark 6. Spoon the mashed potatoes into a piping bag fitted with a wide ridged nozzle and pipe out 18 rosettes on a baking sheet. Melt the remaining butter, brush each rosette, then cook in the oven for 20 minutes.

Patatas Bravas

Serves 4

5 potatoes, peeled and cut into 2.5cm
  cubes
Salt
6 tablespoons olive oil
1 red onion, chopped
3 cloves garlic, chopped
1 tablespoon paprika
Pinch or more of chilli flakes
400g can chopped tomatoes
1 tablespoon chopped fresh oregano

1 Parboil the potatoes in a saucepan of boiling salted water for 5 minutes, then drain well.

2 Heat 4 tablespoons oil in a large frying pan. Add the potatoes and fry slowly for 15 minutes over a medium heat. Transfer the potatoes to an ovenproof serving dish and keep warm in a moderate oven.

3 Heat the remaining oil in the frying pan. Add the onion and garlic and cook for 10 minutes until golden. Add the paprika and chilli flakes and cook for a further 2 minutes. Drain most of the excess juice from the tomatoes, then add them to the fried onion mixture. Cook for 5 minutes, then stir in the oregano. Pour the tomato sauce over the potatoes and serve.

Leek & Potato Layer

Serves 4

4 large potatoes, thinly sliced
2 tablespoons fennel seeds
3 tablespoons extra virgin olive oil
2 leeks, thinly sliced
3 cloves garlic, chopped
Salt and freshly ground black pepper
6 tomatoes, skinned and thinly sliced
15g chopped fresh parsley
2 tablespoons freshly grated Parmesan
   cheese
2 tablespoons dried white
   breadcrumbs
225g mozzarella cheese, chopped

1 Preheat the oven to 180°C/350°F/Gas mark 4. Put the potatoes in a large saucepan and cover with boiling water. Boil for 2 minutes and drain.

2 Rinse and dry the pan, then place the fennel seeds in it. Roast over a gentle heat until they are aromatic, then add the olive oil, leeks and garlic with plenty of salt and pepper. Stir the mixture well and cook over a medium heat for about 10 minutes, or until the leeks are softened.

3 Put a layer of the boiled potatoes in a deep ovenproof dish. Top with a little of the leek mixture, a layer of tomatoes and a sprinkling of parsley. Continue layering the potatoes with the leeks and tomatoes until all are used, ending with a layer of potatoes. Cover and cook in the oven for 45 minutes.

4 Mix the Parmesan with the breadcrumbs and mozzarella cheese. Sprinkle this evenly over the top of the vegetables and return the dish to the oven, uncovered, for a further 30 minutes, or until the topping is crisp and golden. Leave to stand to cool slightly for 5 minutes before serving.

Spiced Grilled
Sweet Potatoes

Serves 4

4 medium sweet potatoes (about 675g)
2 tablespoons olive oil
1 teaspoon crushed chillies
½ teaspoon ground cinnamon
2 cloves garlic, crushed
Salt and freshly ground black pepper

1 Preheat the barbecue grill to medium direct heat.

2 Cut the sweet potatoes, without peeling them, lengthways into 8 wedges each. Put the remaining ingredients into a large bowl and mix together. Season to taste with salt and pepper. Add the potato wedges and mix gently until coated in the spices and oil.

3 Grill the potato wedges, cut-side down over direct heat for 8-10 minutes, turning once, until tender and golden. Watch the potatoes carefully – they can burn very easily because of their high sugar content. Serve immediately.

Tip
Their delicious sweetness makes these potatoes wonderfully versatile, not only in soups and casseroles, but also in sweet dishes, breads and in puddings.

Latkes

Makes about 24

675g potatoes, peeled and coarsely
  grated
1 egg, beaten
Salt and freshly ground black pepper
3 tablespoons plain flour
Sunflower oil, for frying
Soured cream or apple sauce, to serve

1 Put the potatoes in a sieve and rinse under cold running water, then squeeze the moisture out of them. Transfer to a bowl, and add the egg with plenty of salt and pepper. Stir in the flour.

2 Heat a little oil in a frying pan. Stir the potato mixture, then put a spoonful in the pan, and quickly spread the grated potatoes into an evenly thick round. Repeat with more mixture, adding as many pancakes as will comfortably fit in the pan with a little space in between.

3 Cook over a medium heat until the pancakes are crisp and golden underneath. Turn and cook the other side until crisp and golden. Use a spatula to remove the pancakes from the pan, and drain individually on kitchen paper. Keep the pancakes hot until all the remaining mixture is cooked. Serve with soured cream or apple sauce.

New England

Potato Salad

Serves 4

675g waxy new potatoes, halved if
  large
Salt and freshly ground black pepper
3 sticks celery, finely diced
2 spring onions, finely sliced
1 red pepper, seeded and finely diced
225g mayonnaise
150ml soured cream
2 tablespoons chopped fresh parsley

1 Cook the potatoes in a large saucepan of boiling salted water for 15–20 minutes until just soft. Drain well and cut into small pieces. Put in a large bowl with the celery, spring onions and pepper.

2 Mix the mayonnaise with the soured cream and season with salt and pepper, then spoon the mixture over the potato salad. Mix well until all the ingredients are thoroughly coated and lightly stir in the parsley. Leave to chill until ready to serve.

Succotash

Serves 4

175g dried butter beans, soaked
   overnight in cold water
2 tablespoons butter
4 thick bacon rashers, chopped
1 large onion, halved and thinly sliced
1 green pepper, seeded and chopped
600g sweetcorn kernels
120ml chicken or vegetable stock
Salt and freshly ground black pepper
60ml single cream
2 tablespoons chopped fresh coriander

Tip
Butter beans are sweet with a soft, floury texture when cooked. They are very good added to mixed bean salads and rich, meaty stews.

1 Drain the beans and put them in a large saucepan. Add plenty of water and bring to the boil, then boil for 10 minutes. Reduce the heat, cover the pan and simmer the beans for 40 minutes, or until they are tender. Drain in a colander.

2 Add the butter and bacon to the pan and cook until the bacon has just changed colour. Stir in the onion and pepper and cook for 10 minutes, or until the onion is softened, but not browned. Stir frequently during cooking.

3 Add the sweetcorn and the stock, then bring to the boil and reduce the heat. Cover the pan and simmer the sweetcorn for 3 minutes. Add the drained beans but do not mix them in. Cover the pan and simmer for a further 5 minutes, or until the sweetcorn becomes tender.

4 Add salt and pepper to taste and mix the sweetcorn and beans. Stir in the cream and heat for a few seconds without boiling, then add the coriander and mix lightly. Serve at once.

Grilled Corn Cobs

with Flavoured Butter

Serves 4

120g unsalted butter, softened
1 hot green chilli, seeded and finely
    chopped
½ teaspoon ground cumin
1 teaspoon ground coriander
2 tablespoons chopped fresh
    coriander, plus coriander leaves
    to garnish
Salt and freshly ground black pepper
8 corn cobs, husks intact

Tip
If you cannot find
husked corn, wrap the
corn in foil after
spreading with butter.

1 Preheat the barbecue grill to medium direct heat.

2 Put the butter into a medium bowl and beat with a fork or wooden spoon until smooth. Add the chilli, cumin, coriander, chopped coriander and salt and pepper. Mix together thoroughly. Set aside.

3 Carefully peel back the husks of the corn, without removing them. Pull off the silk threads, removing as much as possible. Spread each cob with about 2 tablespoons of the butter mixture, then carefully fold the husk back up over each cob. Tie securely with string at the top.

4 Grill the corn over direct medium heat for 8-10 minutes, turning occasionally, until the corn is lightly and evenly browned.

5 Peel off the husks, garnish with coriander leaves and serve at once.

Sweet Potato Casserole
with Marshmallow Topping

Serves 6

8 medium sweet potatoes
45g dark brown sugar
30g butter
Freshly grated nutmeg, to taste
¾ teaspoon ground cinnamon
¾ teaspoon ground allspice
Freshly squeezed juice of ½ orange
Salt and freshly ground black pepper
Marshmallows, for topping

1 Peel the sweet potatoes and put them in a large saucepan or casserole. Cover with cold water and bring to the boil over a high heat. Reduce the heat to medium and simmer for about 30 minutes, or until the potatoes are tender. Drain and transfer to a large bowl.

2 Meanwhile, preheat the oven to 190°C/375°F/ Gas mark 5. Using a potato masher, mash the potatoes until smooth. Alternatively, put the potatoes through a potato ricer or food mill, or beat with a hand-held electric mixer. Add the sugar, butter, nutmeg to taste, cinnamon, allspice, orange juice, and salt and pepper, and beat until smooth and well blended.

3 Spoon the mixture into a 1.5 litre baking dish and arrange the marshmallows in rows across the surface, pressing them gently into the potato mixture. Bake for 10-15 minutes, or until the potatoes are bubbling and the marshmallows are golden and soft.

Braised Fennel

Serves 4

2 tablespoons butter
1 small onion, finely chopped
1 small carrot, finely chopped
Salt and freshly ground black pepper
4 bulbs fennel, halved lengthways
475ml medium dry white wine

1 Preheat the oven to 200°C/400°F/Gas mark 6. Melt the butter in a casserole. Add the onion and carrot, season with salt and pepper and cook, stirring, for 5 minutes.

2 Add the fennel to the casserole, flat-side down and cook for 2 minutes, then pour in the wine. Heat until simmering, basting the fennel with the wine. Cover and transfer to the oven. Cook about 40 minutes, turning the fennel after 30 minutes, until the bulbs are completely tender. Taste and adjust the seasoning before serving.

Tip

Fennel has a pronounced aniseed flavour – grill meat or fish on top of the leaves so that the fragrance is absorbed as the meat cooks.

Braised Sugar Snaps
with Lettuce

Serves 4

2 tablespoons butter
1 small onion, finely chopped
3 tablespoons chopped fresh tarragon
450g sugar snap peas
Salt and freshly ground black pepper
120ml medium-dry white wine
1 small Little Gem lettuce heart, finely
   shredded
1 spring onion, finely chopped
4 large fresh basil sprigs

1 Melt the butter in a large saucepan. Add the onion, stir well and cover the pan. Cook gently for 5 minutes, then stir in the tarragon and sugar snap peas. Add salt and pepper to taste, and stir in the wine. Heat until just simmering, then cover the pan and cook gently for 5 minutes.

2 Stir in the shredded lettuce, cover the pan again and simmer for a further 3 minutes, or until the lettuce has just wilted and the peas are tender, but still crisp.

3 Taste the sugar snap peas and add more seasoning if necessary, then stir in the spring onion. Use scissors to shred the basil sprigs into the pan, cutting them finely and including the soft stalks with the leaves. Immediately remove from the heat and serve at once, stirring well so that the basil is thoroughly blended into the vegetables as they are served.

Stir-fried Greens
with Shiitake Mushrooms

Serves 4–6

1 tablespoon vegetable oil

3 spring onions, sliced

2.5cm piece fresh root ginger, peeled and finely chopped

3 cloves garlic, crushed

12 shiitake mushrooms, sliced

60ml light soy sauce

1 tablespoon honey or sugar

1 teaspoon toasted sesame oil

3 tablespoons rice wine or sherry

900g fresh mixed greens (such as spinach, mustard greens, collard greens, pak choi or Swiss chard), stems discarded

1 teaspoon toasted sesame seeds, to garnish

1 Heat the oil in a wok or large frying pan. Add half the spring onions, the ginger and garlic and stir-fry for 1 minute. Add the mushrooms and stir-fry for 2 minutes. Add the soy sauce, honey or sugar, sesame oil and rice wine or sherry, and bring to the boil. Cook for 1 minute.

2 Add the mixed greens and stir-fry for about 30 seconds until they become slightly wilted. Using a slotted spoon, remove the vegetables from the wok and transfer to a serving dish.

3 Pour any sauce left in the wok or pan over the vegetables. Sprinkle with the remaining spring onions and the sesame seeds and serve.

Broad Beans

with Prosciutto

Serves 4

4 fresh savory or thyme sprigs
Salt and freshly ground black pepper
1.3kg young broad beans, shelled (they
   yield just over 450g of beans)
1 tablespoon extra virgin olive oil
115g prosciutto, cut into fine strips
2 tablespoons mild onion
2 tablespoons chopped fresh savory or
   thyme leaves
Lemon wedges, to serve (optional)

Tip
Savory and broad beans
go well together – they are
often grown next to each
other as the herb helps to
keep away blackfly.

1 Place the savory or thyme sprigs in a saucepan of salted water and bring to the boil. Add the broad beans. Bring back to the boil and cook for about 5 minutes, or until the beans are tender.

2 Meanwhile, heat the olive oil in a non-stick frying pan. Sprinkle the strips of prosciutto evenly over the pan and cook for about 2 minutes, until the prosciutto is crisp. Transfer the prosciutto and its cooking oil to a large serving bowl. Add the onion and savory or thyme leaves.

3 Drain the beans, discard the herb sprigs, then add them to the prosciutto. Mix well, then add a little salt, if necessary, and plenty of freshly ground black pepper. Toss well and serve at once.

4 Offer lemon wedges with the beans if they are served as the main dish for a light meal or first course, so that the juice can be added to taste.

Potato & Beetroot Mash

Serves 4–6

1kg potatoes, peeled and cut into
   chunks
Salt and freshly ground black pepper
Butter, to taste
60ml natural yoghurt
450g cooked beetroot, coarsely grated
1 small onion, very finely chopped

1 Cook the potatoes in a large saucepan of boiling salted water for about 10 minutes, or until tender. Drain well, then return to the pan.

2 Add butter to taste and the yoghurt, then mash until smooth. Beat in the beetroot and onion, then return the pan to the heat and stir for 2-3 minutes until thoroughly reheated. Add salt and pepper to taste and serve at once.

Carrots

with Maple Syrup

Serves 4

2 tablespoons butter
About 120ml water
8 carrots, cut into even-sized pieces,
   about 5cm long
2 tablespoons maple syrup
Small bunch of fresh parsley, finely
   chopped

1 Melt the butter in a large saucepan and pour in the water. You need roughly 1cm in the bottom of the pan. Add the carrots and stir well to coat them in liquid. Cover and simmer for 12-15 minutes.

2 Remove the lid, increase the heat and bubble to reduce the liquid to about 2 tablespoons. Add the maple syrup, stir and bubble for 1 minute. Stir in the chopped parsley and serve immediately.

Brussels Sprouts
with Sweet Potatoes

Serves 4

450g sweet potato, peeled
350g small Brussels sprouts
Salt and freshly ground black pepper
2 tablespoons extra virgin olive oil
Pinch of ground cloves
Good pinch of ground mace
½ teaspoon dried oregano or
   marjoram
1 teaspoon sugar
Grated zest and juice of 1 large orange

1 Cut the sweet potato into chunks about the same size as the Brussels sprouts. Add the sweet potatoes to a large saucepan of boiling salted water and bring back just to boiling point. Cook for 2 minutes.

2 Add the Brussels sprouts to the pan and bring back to the boil. Reduce the heat, if necessary, so that the water does not boil too fiercely and break up the sweet potato, then cook for 5 minutes until the sweet potato and sprouts are tender, but not too soft. Drain in a colander.

3 Return the pan to the heat and add the olive oil, herbs and spices, sugar and orange zest and juice. Whisk over a high heat until the mixture boils. Boil hard, still whisking, for about 30 seconds. Add salt and pepper to taste.

4 Remove the pan from the heat and return the vegetables to it. Carefully turn them in the orange mixture to coat them evenly, taking care not to break up the delicate pieces of sweet potato and the sprouts. Serve immediately.

Hot Vegetable Salad

Serves 4

28 small new potatoes, scrubbed
Salt and freshly ground black pepper
16 baby carrots, scrubbed
100g shelled or frozen peas
Handful of fresh parsley sprigs
Handful of fresh mint sprigs
Handful of fresh dill sprigs
1 teaspoon sugar
1 tablespoon whole-grain mustard
2 tablespoons balsamic vinegar
5 tablespoons extra virgin olive oil
8 spring onions, chopped
1–2 cos lettuce hearts, shredded

1 Put the potatoes in a large saucepan and pour in boiling water to cover. Add a little salt, then bring to the boil. Reduce the heat, cover and simmer for 10 minutes. Add the carrots and peas and bring back to the boil, then reduce the heat again. Cover and keep the vegetables just boiling for a further 5 minutes until the potatoes and vegetables are cooked.

2 Meanwhile, place the parsley, mint, dill and sugar in a food processor and process until finely chopped. Add the mustard, vinegar, salt and pepper, then process again until well mixed. Pour in the olive oil and process for a few seconds. Turn into a bowl and stir in the spring onions.

3 Drain the vegetables and add them to the dressing, then toss well to coat them evenly. Arrange the lettuce in a large shallow dish and pile in the vegetable salad. Serve at once.

Spiced Courgettes

Serves 4

2 tablespoons butter
1 onion, finely chopped
8 green cardamom pods
2 teaspoons cumin seeds
1 bay leaf
675g courgettes, peeled, halved and
    seeded, cut into 2.5cm chunks
Salt and freshly ground black pepper
240ml coconut milk
120ml Greek yoghurt or crème fraîche
2 spring onions, finely chopped
2 tablespoons chopped fresh coriander

1 Melt the butter in a saucepan. Add the onion.

2 Add the cardamom, making a slit in each pod and crushing it slightly as you add it to the pan. Stir in the cumin seeds and bay leaf, then cover the pan, and cook gently for 15 minutes.

3 Stir in the courgettes with salt and pepper to taste. Continue stirring until the courgettes are thoroughly combined with the onion and spices. Then pour in the coconut milk and heat until simmering. Simmer, uncovered, for 15 minutes, or until the courgettes are tender. Stir the courgettes frequently so that the pieces cook evenly.

4 Stir in the yoghurt or crème fraîche and immediately remove the pan from the heat. Add more seasoning, if necessary. Remove the bay leaf and serve immediately, sprinkled with the spring onions and fresh coriander.

Roasted Vegetables

with Pine Nuts & Parmesan

Serves 4

4 tablespoons olive oil

8 small new potatoes, halved or
quartered lengthways, if large

4 small parsnips, halved or quartered
lengthways, if large

Salt and freshly ground black pepper

6 baby leeks, trimmed

4 asparagus spears, trimmed

50g freshly grated Parmesan cheese

2 tablespoons pine nuts, toasted

10g fresh white breadcrumbs

1 Preheat the oven to 200°C/400°F/Gas mark 6.
Pour the oil into a roasting tin, add the potatoes
and parsnips and toss well to coat in the oil.
Season with salt and pepper and roast in the oven
for 30 minutes.

2 Add the leeks and asparagus to the roasting tin.
Toss all the vegetables together, return to the
oven and roast for a further 25 minutes.

3 Mix together the Parmesan cheese, pine nuts
and breadcrumbs.

4 Sprinkle the mixture over the roasted
vegetables and cook for a further 5 minutes
until crispy and golden.

Cauliflower & Leek

Patties

Makes 8 patties

2 tablespoons olive oil
2 leeks, finely chopped
1 clove garlic, crushed
1 teaspoon dried marjoram
350g cauliflower (including the stalk and any little green leaves), finely chopped
Salt and freshly ground black pepper
100g fresh white breadcrumbs
15g chopped fresh parsley
4 spring onions, chopped
100g grated Cheddar cheese

1 Heat the oil in a saucepan. Add the leeks, garlic and marjoram. Stir for 5 minutes, or until the leeks are softened slightly, then add the cauliflower and stir well. Cover and cook for 5 minutes. Stir in the seasoning, then cook, uncovered, for a further 5 minutes, stirring occasionally. Turn the vegetables into a bowl and leave to cool.

2 Mix in the breadcrumbs, parsley, spring onions and cheese. Taste for seasoning and add more salt and pepper, if required. Cover a baking tray with cling film, shape the mixture into 8 round patties and place them on the baking tray as they are ready. Cover loosely with cling film and chill for 1 hour.

3 Preheat the grill. Place the patties on a flameproof dish, or line the grill pan with foil and brush it lightly with oil, then place the patties on it. Brush the patties with a little oil and grill for 3-4 minutes, or until golden brown on top. Turn the patties, brush with oil and cook until golden for 3-4 minutes on the second side. Serve at once.

Maple-baked Acorn Squash

Serves 4

2 medium acorn squash
2 tablespoons butter
60ml pure natural maple syrup
¼ teaspoon salt
¼ teaspoon ground cinnamon
⅛ teaspoon allspice
40g chopped pecan nuts or walnuts
  (optional)

Tip
Acorn squash can be stuffed with spiced mincemeat, or boiled then mashed with plenty of black pepper and butter.

1 Preheat the oven to 180°C/350°F/Gas mark 4. Cut each squash in half lengthways, then scoop out their seeds and fibres. Use a sharp knife to slice off a small piece of each base. Arrange the squash halves, cut-side down, in an ovenproof dish and cover with foil. Bake for about 30 minutes, or until the squash begins to soften.

2 Turn the squash cut-side up and divide the butter, maple syrup, salt and spices equally among them. Sprinkle each one with nuts, if using. Bake, uncovered, for about 20 minutes, or until the squash are tender.

Mexican Pot Beans

Serves 4-6

500g dried pinto beans
1 onion, finely chopped
75g smoked bacon, chopped
2 dried red chillies, roughly chopped
2 cloves garlic, roughly chopped
1 bay leaf, crumbled
1 tablespoon salt
Freshly ground black pepper, to taste

1 Put the pinto beans into a large bowl and pick them over, removing any little stones or beans that are shrivelled or discoloured. Cover the beans with at least twice their volume of cold water and leave to soak overnight.

2 Next day, drain the beans and put into a large saucepan (one that is tall and deep is best as it will reduce evaporation of water). Add the onion, bacon, chillies, garlic and bay leaf and cover with water by about 7.5-10cm (about 1.5-2 litres).

3 Bring slowly to the boil, skimming off any residue that rises to the surface. When boiling, reduce the heat, cover and simmer very gently for 2 hours.

4 Add the salt and continue to cook the beans, uncovered, for another 1 hour, or until they are very tender and the liquid is very thick. Taste for seasoning and add more salt, if necessary, and black pepper. Serve immediately or cool and refrigerate for up to 3 days.

Classic Healthy Coleslaw

Serves 4

150ml good quality mayonnaise

150ml natural yoghurt or crème
    fraîche

1 teaspoon Dijon mustard

Salt and freshly ground black pepper

3 tablespoons chopped fresh parsley

3 tablespoons raisins

225g green cabbage, finely shredded

1 large carrot, coarsely grated

½ small onion, finely chopped

1 First make the mayonnaise dressing in a large bowl, big enough to mix the salad. Mix the mayonnaise with the yoghurt or crème fraîche. Add the mustard, plenty of salt and pepper and the parsley. Stir well so that all the flavours are fully blended.

2 Add the raisins to the dressing and mix well. Then add the cabbage, carrot and onion. Mix the ingredients thoroughly until they are combined and coated with dressing. Taste and add salt and pepper as necessary.

3 Cover the coleslaw and chill for at least 1 hour, then remove from the refrigerator for 15–20 minutes before serving. The salad tastes best when made and chilled a day in advance – the flavours mingle and mellow, and the raisins plump up and impart a gentle sweetness to the salad.

Spinach & Mushroom
Salad with Hot Bacon Dressing

Serves 4

450g baby spinach leaves, washed and
dried

120g white mushrooms, thinly sliced

2 tablespoons vegetable oil or bacon
fat

4 rindless bacon rashers, cut into thin
shreds

4 spring onions, thinly sliced,
or 2 tablespoons snipped chives

1 clove garlic, crushed

250ml cider vinegar or wine vinegar

½ teaspoon salt

½ teaspoon dry mustard powder

Freshly ground black pepper, to taste

1 Toss the spinach leaves and sliced mushrooms in a large, heatproof salad bowl. Heat the oil or bacon fat in a heavy-based frying-pan over medium heat. Add the bacon and cook until crisp and brown, stirring frequently. Drain on kitchen paper.

2 Add the spring onions and garlic to the pan and cook over a low heat until softened, stirring frequently. Stir in the vinegar, salt and dry mustard, and season with black pepper. Bring to the boil, and carefully pour over the leaves. Sprinkle the bacon on top and toss lightly to mix. Serve immediately.

Caesar Salad

Serves 6

1 egg, at room temperature

4–7 tablespoons olive oil

15g butter

1 clove garlic, crushed

75–115g French bread, cut into small cubes

2 tablespoons lemon juice

Freshly ground black pepper, to taste

1 large or 2 small heads cos lettuce, torn into bite-sized pieces

4 tablespoons freshly grated Parmesan cheese, plus long curls or shreds to garnish

3 good quality anchovy fillets, cut up (optional)

1 To coddle the egg, bring a small saucepan of water to the boil over a high heat. Carefully slide the egg into the water and remove the pan from the heat. Cover and leave to stand for 1 minute.

2 Heat 1-2 tablespoons oil and the butter in a medium frying pan over a medium-high heat. Add the garlic and bread cubes and cook for 2-3 minutes, tossing and stirring, until the bread is golden on all sides. Remove from the heat and set the croûtons aside.

3 Put the lemon juice in a large salad bowl and add 3-5 tablespoons oil. Crack the egg into the bowl and whisk it into the lemon juice and oil until blended and creamy. Season with pepper, then add the lettuce and grated Parmesan and toss to coat. Add the anchovies, if using. Sprinkle over the croûtons. Garnish with Parmesan curls or shreds and serve.

Chickpea & Tomato
Salad

Serves 3–4

1 clove garlic, crushed
Juice of 1 lemon
1 tablespoon tahini
3 tablespoons extra virgin olive oil
2 tablespoons chopped fresh mint
2 tablespoons chopped fresh coriander
1 tablespoon chopped fresh parsley
12 cherry tomatoes, halved
1 small red onion, finely chopped
400g can chickpeas, rinsed
Salt and freshly ground black pepper

1 Whisk the garlic, lemon juice, tahini, olive oil and chopped herbs together in a medium bowl.

2 Stir in the tomatoes, onion and chickpeas, and season to taste with salt and pepper.

Tip
Chickpeas have a rich, nutty flavour and are ideal in casseroles, soups and stews, as well as providing body for salads.

Waldorf Salad

Serves 4

4 sticks celery, thinly sliced
2 large red apples, quartered, cored
  and diced
120g walnuts, chopped
120g chopped soft dates or figs
  (optional)
About 225g mayonnaise
Lettuce leaves
Pecan nut halves or apple slices, to
  garnish

1 Combine the celery, apples and walnuts in a bowl, and the dates or figs, if using. Gradually stir in enough mayonnaise to hold all the ingredients together.

2 Arrange the lettuce leaves on a plate and heap the salad on them. Garnish with pecan halves or apple slices.

Chef's Salad

Serves 4

2 heads soft or butterhead lettuce, trimmed

225g honey-baked ham, cut into strips

225g cooked chicken or turkey breast, cut into strips

225g Emmental or Cheddar cheese, cut into strips

8 cherry tomatoes, quartered

4 hard-boiled eggs, quartered

For the dressing

2 tablespoons lemon juice or white wine vinegar

1 tablespoon Dijon mustard

Salt and freshly ground black pepper

1 clove garlic, crushed

1 teaspoon sugar (optional)

60ml vegetable oil

2–3 tablespoons extra virgin olive oil

1 To make the dressing, put the lemon juice or white wine vinegar in a small bowl with the mustard, salt and pepper, garlic and sugar, if using. Stir to blend well. Slowly pour in the vegetable oil in a thin stream, whisking continuously until a smooth, creamy dressing begins to form. Continue whisking while adding the olive oil in the same way until the dressing is thick and smooth. Set aside.

2 Leave any small lettuce leaves whole and tear large leaves into smaller pieces, then divide evenly among 4 individual salad bowls or place on a large shallow platter.

3 Arrange the ham, chicken or turkey, and cheese strips on top of the lettuce, radiating from the middle to resemble wheel spokes and keeping even spaces between each ingredient. Fill the spaces with the tomato and egg quarters. Drizzle the salad dressing over and serve.

Panzanella

Serves 6–8

1 small ciabatta or rustic loaf, about 175g, cut into cubes

1 cucumber, peeled, seeded and coarsely chopped

4 ripe tomatoes, halved and cut into chunks

2 tablespoons capers, rinsed

For the dressing

2 cloves garlic

2 tablespoons red wine vinegar

8 tablespoons olive oil

Salt and freshly ground black pepper

2 hard-boiled eggs, coarsely chopped

8–10 fresh basil leaves

1 Preheat the oven to 200°C/400°F/Gas mark 6. Place the bread cubes on a baking tray and toast in the oven for 10 minutes. Transfer to a high-sided salad bowl.

2 Add the cucumber and tomatoes to the salad bowl. Sprinkle with the capers.

3 To make the dressing, pound the garlic cloves in a mortar with a pestle. Whisk in the vinegar and oil, and season with salt and pepper. Pour the dressing over the salad.

4 Arrange the hard-boiled eggs on top of the salad with the basil leaves. Leave to stand for 15 minutes, then stir once before serving – you want the bread to soak up the juices and dressing but not become unappealingly soggy.

Roasted Tomato &

Goat's Cheese Salad

Serves 4–6

6 plum tomatoes, halved lengthways
4 tablespoons olive oil
1 teaspoon chopped fresh rosemary
2 tablespoons chopped fresh basil,
  plus extra to garnish
1 tablespoon balsamic vinegar
1 shallot, finely chopped
Salt and freshly ground black pepper
100g fresh goat's cheese
Bread, to serve

1 Preheat the grill to high. Arrange the tomato halves, cut-side up, on a grill pan or baking tray. Mix 1 tablespoon of the oil with the rosemary. Brush this mixture over the tomatoes. Transfer to the grill and cook for 6–8 minutes until the tomatoes are softened and starting to char round the edges. Remove from the heat and transfer the tomatoes to a large serving dish with any juices.

2 Mix the remaining oil with the basil, balsamic vinegar and shallot. Pour this mixture over the tomatoes and season with some salt and pepper. Leave to cool to room temperature.

3 Divide the tomatoes among 4 or 6 serving plates and top each one with a spoonful of goat's cheese, drizzling over some of the dressing. Garnish with some fresh basil leaves and serve with plenty of bread.

Green Bean &

Mozzarella Salad

Serves 4

350g fine green beans
350g mozzarella cheese, thinly sliced

For the dressing
3 tablespoons coriander seeds
Grated zest and juice of 1 large orange
1 tablespoon cider vinegar
½ teaspoon sugar
1 teaspoon whole-grain mustard
1 small clove garlic, chopped
Salt and freshly ground black pepper
5 tablespoons extra virgin olive oil
3 tablespoons chopped fresh parsley

1 To make the dressing, roast the coriander seeds in a small, heavy-based saucepan over a medium heat. Shake the pan frequently until the seeds begin to smell aromatic and darken very slightly. Tip the coriander seeds into a mortar as soon as they are roasted – do not leave them in the pan or they may overcook, becoming dark and bitter. Use a pestle to crush the seeds coarsely.

2 In a bowl large enough to hold the beans, mix the seeds with the orange zest and juice, cider vinegar, sugar, mustard and garlic. Season with salt and pepper. Whisk until the sugar and salt have dissolved, then whisk in the olive oil to make a slightly thickened dressing. Add the parsley.

3 Cook the green beans in a large saucepan of boiling water for about 3 minutes until crisp but not soft. Drain and immediately add them to the dressing. Turn the beans in the dressing to cool them quickly. Cover and leave to marinate for about 1 hour, if possible, or at least until they are cold.

4 Add the mozzarella to the beans and mix the salad gently, taking care not to break up the cheese. Spoon on to individual plates and serve.

Stir-fried Brown Rice

& Vegetables

Serves 4

430g short-grain brown rice
1 litre cold water
Pinch of salt
115g sesame seeds
Small handful of dried arame seaweed
Sesame oil
2 onions, finely diced
2 teaspoons soy sauce
2 carrots, sliced into batons
5mm strips nori seaweed or finely
chopped fresh parsley, to garnish

1 Wash the rice under cold running water, to allow any debris or chaff to overflow. Combine the rice with the cold water and salt in a heavy-based saucepan. Bring to a rapid boil without the lid, then cover and reduce the heat. Cook for 30–35 minutes until tender.

2 Meanwhile, wash the sesame seeds in a sieve under cold running water, then empty into a heavy-base frying pan and cook over a medium heat, stirring, until they turn golden brown and a few of them begin to pop and crackle. Remove and leave to cool.

3 Soak the arame seaweed in a bowl of water for 5-6 minutes. Remove the arame from the water and squeeze out any excess liquid.

4 Cover the surface of a clean heavy-based frying pan with sesame oil and heat. Add the onions with half the soy sauce and sauté until they are translucent. Add the carrots and continue to stir. Add the arame seaweed to the onions and carrots then stir-fry 2 minutes.

5 Slowly add the cooked brown rice to the pan and stir to prevent the mixture from sticking. If you feel the dish needs more liquid, add the water used for soaking the arame. Continue stirring until the rice is hot. Add the remaining soy sauce during the final minute, and mix in the sesame seeds. Garnish wih nori seaweed or finely chopped parsley and serve immediately.

Texas Pilaf

Serves 4

320g basmati or Texmati rice
1 tablespoon olive oil
1 onion, finely chopped
1 green chilli, seeded and finely
    chopped
1 clove garlic, finely chopped
2 teaspoons cumin seeds
1 large tomato, skinned and roughly
    chopped
500ml chicken stock
2 tablespoons chopped fresh coriander
Salt and freshly ground black pepper,
    to taste

1 Put the rice into a large bowl. Pour in plenty of cold water, then swirl the grains gently, let them settle and pour off the cloudy water. Repeat this process several times until the water runs clear. Put the rice into a sieve and leave to drain while you prepare the remaining ingredients.

2 Heat the oil in a large saucepan or casserole with a tight-fitting lid over a medium heat. When hot, add the onion, chilli and garlic. Cook, stirring occasionally, for 5-7 minutes until the onion begins to brown. Add the cumin seeds and stir for a further 30 seconds or so.

3 Add the tomato and cook for another 1 minute until softened. Add the drained rice and stir well to coat in the oil and tomato.

4 Add the stock and bring to the boil. Reduce the heat as low as possible and cover tightly. Simmer over the lowest heat for 15 minutes, then remove from the heat and leave to stand without lifting the lid for a further 10 minutes.

5 Just before serving, add the coriander and season to taste with salt and pepper.

Broccoli Pilaf

Serves 4

200g basmati rice
450g small broccoli florets
2 tablespoons sunflower oil
2 onions, thinly sliced
2 cloves garlic, crushed
2 sticks celery, thinly sliced
2 tablespoons cumin seeds
8 green cardamom pods
1 bay leaf
1 cinnamon stick
Salt and freshly ground black pepper
1 teaspoon saffron threads
2 tablespoons boiling water

1 Put the basmati rice in a bowl. Pour in plenty of cold water, then swirl the grains gently, let them settle and pour off the cloudy water. Repeat this process several times until the water runs clear. Cover with fresh cold water and set aside to soak for 30 minutes.

2 Cook the broccoli in a large saucepan of boiling water for 2 minutes. Drain the broccoli, reserving the vegetable stock.

3 Heat the oil in a frying pan. Add the onions, garlic, celery, cumin seeds, cardamom pods, bay leaf and cinnamon stick. Stir, then cook 10 minutes stirring occasionally, until the onions have softened and are beginning to brown.

4 Meanwhile, drain the rice and set it aside in the sieve. When the onions are cooked, add the rice to the pan and pour in the reserved stock. Add salt and pepper, then bring to the boil over a high heat and stir once. Cover the pan and reduce the heat to the lowest setting. Cook for 10 minutes.

5 While the rice is cooking, pound the saffron threads in a mortar with a pestle and stir in the boiling water. Sprinkle the saffron water over the rice, then add the broccoli, leaving it piled on top of the rice. Quickly re-cover the pan and cook for another 5 minutes. Remove from the heat and leave to stand, without removing the lid, for 3 minutes. Fluff the rice with a fork and mix in the broccoli. Serve immediately.

Coconut Rice

Serves 4

350g Thai jasmine rice
400ml coconut milk
120ml water
1 teaspoon salt

1 Put the rice into a large bowl. Pour in plenty of cold water, then swirl the grains gently, let them settle and pour off the cloudy water. Repeat this process several times until the water runs clear. Put the rice into a sieve and leave to drain.

2 Put the rice into a large saucepan with the coconut milk and water. Add the salt and stir well. Cover and bring to the boil. As soon as the liquid comes up to the boil, reduce the heat as low as possible and cook for 10 minutes.

3 Remove from the heat and leave to stand for a further 10 minutes. Do not lift the lid until the entire 20 minutes have elapsed. Fluff up with a fork before serving.

Egg-fried Rice

Serves 4

1 tablespoon vegetable oil
500g cold cooked rice
50g chopped bacon
115g thawed frozen peas
8 eggs, beaten
8 tablespoons soy sauce
8 spring onions, finely chopped

1 Heat a wok over a high heat until smoking. Add the oil and swirl around the pan. Add the cold cooked rice and stir-fry for 1 minute.

2 Add the bacon and peas. Continue to cook for 5 minutes. Add the eggs and cook for a further 2 minutes. Add the soy sauce and remove from the heat. Stir in the spring onions and serve immediately.

Emmental & Roasted

Corn Spoon Bread

Serves 4

3 corn cobs
3 tablespoons vegetable oil
120g plain flour
150g cornmeal or instant polenta
1 tablespoon baking powder
½ teaspoon bicarbonate of soda
½ teaspoon salt
2 eggs
250ml buttermilk
55g butter, melted
55g Emmental cheese, grated

1 Preheat the oven to 200°C/400°F/Gas mark 6. Put the corn cobs in a roasting tin and pour over the oil. Roast in the oven for 30 minutes. Leave to cool, then slice off the kernels – you will have about 115g.

2 Mix the flour, cornmeal or polenta, baking powder, bicarbonate of soda and salt together in a large bowl.

3 Add the eggs and buttermilk and beat well. Stir in the melted butter, Emmental and sweetcorn kernels.

4 Preheat the oven to 190°C/375°F/Gas mark 5. Grease and line a 1.2 litre loaf tin. Spoon the mixture in to the prepared tin and bake in the oven for 40–45 minutes, or until a skewer inserted into the centre comes out clean. Set aside for 10 minutes then turn out on to a wire rack. Serve just warm.

Courgette Bread

Makes a 900g loaf

430g plain flour
1 teaspoon salt
2 teaspoons baking powder
2 teaspoons dried thyme
1 courgette, coarsely grated
   (to yield about 300–350g)
3 eggs
60ml extra virgin olive oil
4–6 tablespoons milk

Tip
Courgettes are wonderfully versatile and can be thinly sliced and quickly fried in olive oil. They are also delicious dipped in batter and deep fried.

1 Preheat the oven to 180°C/350°F/Gas mark 4 and grease a 23 x 13cm loaf tin. Mix the flour, salt, baking powder and thyme together in a bowl. Make a large well in the middle and add the grated courgette. Make another well in the middle of the courgette, but do not mix in.

2 Add the eggs, olive oil and 4 tablespoons of the milk to the well in the courgette. Beat the eggs with the wet ingredients and gradually work in the courgette. Then work in the dry ingredients from the outside of the bowl, adding the remaining 2 tablespoons of milk, if necessary, to make a firm mixture that is also soft enough to drop from the spoon when jerked sharply.

3 Turn the mixture into the loaf tin and press down into the corners. Bake for 45–50 minutes, or until the loaf is well risen and browned on top. Insert a metal skewer into the middle of the bread. If the skewer comes out clean, with no mixture clinging to it, the loaf is cooked. If not, cook for a further 5 minutes and test it again. Turn the loaf out to cool on a wire rack. Serve warm or cool, with butter.

Old-fashioned Cornbread

Serves 6–8

120g butter, cut into cubes
190g yellow cornmeal or
    instant polenta
100g plain flour
55g sugar
1 tablespoon baking powder
½ teaspoon salt
1 egg, lightly beaten
250ml buttermilk
Butter, to serve

1 Preheat the oven to 220°C/425°F/Gas mark 7. Put the butter in a 23–25cm cast-iron frying pan or heavy-based ovenproof dish and put in the oven for 3–5 minutes until the butter has melted. Swirl to coat the inside of the pan.

2 Meanwhile, put the cornmeal or polenta, flour, sugar, baking powder and salt in a large mixing bowl and stir to combine. Make a large well in the middle of the mixture.

3 Set aside 2 tablespoons of the melted butter in a small bowl to cool slightly and pour the remainder into the middle of the dry ingredients. Keep the frying pan or dish warm. Using a fork, beat the egg and buttermilk together in a small bowl and beat in the reserved butter. Pour into the well in the cornmeal mixture and stir gently until just combined; do not overmix. Pour the mixture into the hot frying pan or dish.

4 Bake in the oven for 18–20 minutes, or until the cornbread top is set and golden and a cake tester or metal skewer comes out with just a few crumbs attached when inserted into the middle. Serve hot or warm, with butter.

Bacon & Caramelized
Onion Rolls

Makes 12 rolls

2 tablespoons butter
1 onion, finely chopped
1 teaspoon sugar
1 tablespoon vegetable oil, plus extra
    for brushing
115g lean bacon, finely chopped

For the dough
500g strong plain flour, plus extra
    for dusting
1 teaspoon salt
2 teaspoons fast action dried yeast
300ml milk
1 egg, beaten

1 Melt the butter in a frying pan. Add the onion and sugar and cook over a low heat for 25–30 minutes until the onion is deep golden. Remove and leave to cool.

2 Add the oil and bacon to the frying pan and cook for 5 minutes. Mix the bacon with the onion and set aside until completely cold.

3 Put the flour in a large bowl and stir in the salt and yeast. Heat the milk until it is just hand hot and pour it into the flour. Add the egg, and onion and bacon, then mix together. Turn the dough out onto a well-floured board and knead for 10 minutes. Put the dough in a clean, oiled bowl, cover and leave to rise for 1 hour.

4 Knock back the dough with your fist to deflate, then divide it into 12 even-sized pieces. Knead each piece of dough for 2 minutes, then shape into a roll.

5 Preheat the oven to 220°C/425°F/Gas mark 7. Put the rolls on a large baking tray and brush with oil. Leave to rise for another 20 minutes until doubled in size, then bake in the oven for 10–15 minutes until golden.

6 Remove the rolls from the oven and cover with a damp tea towel until cold – this will give the rolls a soft crust.

DESSERTS

- Berry Ice Lollies
- Mango Ice Cream
- Caramel Ice Cream
- Poached Pears with Maple Syrup & Pecans
- Pumpkin Pie
- Tropical Fruit Salad
- Meringues with Cream & Blueberries
- Spiced Baked Apples
- Sticky Toffee Pudding
- New England Blueberry Pancakes
- Double-crust Apple Pie
- Lychees with Orange & Ginger
- Chocolate Fondue
- Chocolate Mousse
- Chilled Mandarin & Lemon Mousse
- Baked Alaska Birthday Cake
- Apple Sauce Sundae
- Chocolate-chip Muffins
- Chocolate-covered Doughnuts
- Peanut Butter Brownies
- Apple Cake Bars
- Cherry Clafoutis
- Boston Cream Pie
- Stove-top Rice Pudding with Dried Fruit
- Summer Berry Shortcakes

CHAPTER SIX

DESSERTS

Berry Ice Lollies

Makes 6–8

475ml water
450g sugar
450g mixed berries, fresh, canned or
    frozen
Juice of 1 lime

Tip
Use any summer fruits
to make these delicious,
refreshing ice lollies.
Try apricots, peaches
or raspberries.

1 Pour the water into a large saucepan and add the sugar. Bring to the boil and simmer for 2 minutes.

2 Remove the pan from the heat and leave to cool completely.

3 Put the berries in a blender and purée or mash well by hand. Add the lime juice and sugar syrup, and mix well.

4 Pour the mixture into lollipop moulds and leave to freeze overnight.

Mango Ice Cream

Serves 4

150g sugar
3 egg yolks
300ml milk
140ml double cream
2 ripe mangoes (total weight about
    675g)
2 tablespoons fresh orange juice
Fresh mango slices, to serve (optional)

1 Have ready a saucepan and a heatproof bowl that will fit on top of it. Put half the sugar in the bowl and add the egg yolks. Whisk until pale and thick. Half fill the pan with water, making sure the level is below that of the bowl when placed on top. Heat the water to simmering point.

2 Heat the milk and cream in a separate saucepan. When the mixture boils, stir it into the egg yolks. Place the bowl over the simmering water and stir continously until the mixture thickens to a custard that coats the back of a spoon. Leave the custard to cool, stirring it occasionally, then chill.

3 Peel the mangoes. Slice the flesh off each stone and put it in a blender or food processor. Process until smooth, then add the remaining sugar and orange juice. Process briefly to mix.

4 Stir the mango purée into the chilled custard. Churn the mixture in an ice cream maker. Alternatively, cover and freeze for 2 hours. Remove from the freezer and beat the mixture using an electric or balloon whisk until smooth. Repeat freezing and whisking twice, then freeze until firm. The whisking during freezing prevents large ice crystals from forming and ensures that the ice cream is smooth.

5 Let the ice cream soften a little before serving in scoops in ice cream cones, or in bowls, with slices of fresh mango.

Caramel Ice Cream

Serves 6

100g sugar
About 3 tablespoons water
300ml double cream
1 vanilla pod, split lengthways or
    1 teaspoon vanilla extract
300ml milk
5 egg yolks

1 Melt the sugar in a heavy-based saucepan with the water. As soon as the sugar has dissolved, increase the heat and boil until the sugar turns a very dark golden colour – it is important to be bold here, or the ice cream will be too sweet. Carefully swirl the pan if the sugar isn't colouring evenly.

2 As soon as it is a dark mahogany colour, remove from the heat, wait a minute, then pour on the cream, standing well back so you don't get splattered. When the bubbling subsides, stir until smooth.

3 Meanwhile, put the vanilla pod into a saucepan with the milk and bring to the boil, as before. Leave to infuse.

4 Beat the egg yolks until pale, then pour over the milk, discarding the vanilla pod. Return this mixture to a fresh saucepan and, stirring continuously with a wooden spoon, cook over a gentle heat until thickened. Do not allow to boil or the egg will scramble. The custard is ready when the mixture coats the back of a wooden spoon without running off freely.

5 When cooked, add to the caramel and cream mixture, stirring until well blended.

6 Cover and freeze for 2 hours. Remove from the freezer and beat the mixture using an electric or balloon whisk until smooth. Repeat freezing and whisking twice, then freeze until firm. The whisking during freezing prevents large ice crystals from forming and ensures that the ice cream is smooth.

7 Alternatively, use an ice cream machine, following the manufacturer's instructions.

Poached Pears
with Maple Syrup & Pecans

Serves 4

1 lemon
240ml water
6 tablespoons pure maple syrup
1 cinnamon stick
4 firm pears
50g light brown sugar
2 tablespoons butter, diced
300ml double cream
2 egg yolks
Chopped pecan nuts, to decorate

1 Pare a long strip of zest from the lemon and put it in a large saucepan. Squeeze the lemon and set aside 1 tablespoon of the juice. Add the remaining juice to the pan, with the water and 2 tablespoons of the maple syrup. Add the cinnamon stick and heat, stirring gently all the time.

2 Peel the pears, leaving them whole. Add them to the syrup, carefully spoon it over them, then cover the pan. Poach the pears, basting them occasionally, until they are transparent and just tender, but still firm enough to hold their shape well. The timing will depend on the type of pears used, and their size, so check them frequently. When they are cooked, carefully transfer them to a dish and leave them to cool, spooning the syrup over from time to time. When cool, chill until ready to serve.

3 Meanwhile, put the brown sugar in a heavy-based saucepan and add the remaining maple syrup, the reserved lemon juice and the butter. Heat gently, stirring, until the mixture is smooth. Remove the pan from the heat.

4 Heat the cream in a separate saucepan. When it is on the verge of boiling, pour it into the brown sugar mixture in a steady stream, stirring all the time.

5 Beat the egg yolks with 6 tablespoons of the cream mixture. Stir the mixture back into the pan and heat gently, stirring all the time until the sauce starts to thicken.

6 Drain the pears and add them to the maple sauce mixture to warm through gently. Serve the pears with the maple sauce spooned over and decorate with the chopped pecans.

Pumpkin Pie

Serves 4

1 pre-baked 30cm pastry case
Cold single cream, to serve

For the filling
900g pumpkin to yield 675g pumpkin
   pulp, flesh cut into 5cm pieces
2 eggs, beaten
90g soft brown sugar
250ml golden syrup
250ml double cream
2 teaspoons ground cinnamon
1 teaspoon ground ginger
½ teaspoon ground nutmeg
1 teaspoon vanilla extract

1 Preheat the oven to 190°C/375°F/Gas mark 5.
Put the pumpkin in a saucepan and cover with water. Bring to the boil, then simmer for 15 minutes until tender. Drain the pumpkin very well, cool and purée in a blender or food processor. Spoon into a large mixing bowl.

2 Add the eggs, sugar, golden syrup and double cream to the pumpkin purée and mix well. Stir in the spices and vanilla extract. Spoon the mixture into the pastry case and bake in the oven for 30–35 minutes until the filling is firm to the touch. Serve warm with cold single cream.

Tropical Fruit Salad

Serves 4

2.5cm piece fresh root ginger, peeled
  and finely chopped
425ml water
225g sugar
1 star anise
1 stick lemon grass
2 kaffir lime leaves
1 mango
1 papaya
2 Nashi or other firm pears
1 melon, such as Ogen

1 Put the ginger, water and sugar in a large saucepan. Add the star anise, lemon grass and lime leaves. Bring to the boil then simmer quite fiercely for 20 minutes, or until the water has reduced and the liquid is quite syrupy. Remove the lime leaves and lemon grass. Leave to cool.

2 Cut the mango into cubes and put into a mixing bowl.

3 Halve the papaya lengthways and scrape out the seeds. Peel carefully and cut into large cubes. Add to the mixing bowl.

4 Peel the pears and remove the core. Slice quite thickly and stir in with the other fruit.

5 Halve the melon and scrape out the seeds. Quarter and remove the flesh from the rind. Cut into 1cm slices. Put in the mixing bowl. Pour the syrup over the fruit and serve chilled.

Meringues
with Cream & Blueberries

Serves 4

2 egg whites
Pinch of salt
85g caster sugar
Drop of vanilla extract
100ml double cream
250g blueberries

1. Preheat the oven to 120°C/250°F/Gas mark ½. Line a baking tray with greaseproof paper then set aside.

2. Using an electric whisk, beat the egg whites with the salt until stiff. Check this by lifting the whisk from the mixture and holding it upside down. If the tip of the egg white falls, the peak is soft. If it stands firm, it is stiff.

3. Add about half the sugar and whisk thoroughly. Keep whisking until the egg white no longer appears grainy and is very shiny and smooth. Add more sugar, about 1 tablespoon at a time, whisking thoroughly between additions until all of it has been added. Add the vanilla extract. Keep whisking until the mixture is smooth, thick and glossy. If the sugar is not whisked in thoroughly enough, it will melt and leach out during cooking, making a very sticky mess.

4. Place 8 large spoonfuls of the mixture on to the prepared baking sheet, leaving plenty of space in between. Use the back of the spoon to make nice peaks on the tops. Transfer to the oven and cook for 1 hour, then switch off the oven and leave until cold. This will give the meringues a crisp outside and chewy, 'marshmallowy' inside. If you prefer them crisper, cook for 1½ hours then leave until cold.

5. Whip the double cream until soft peaks form. Take one meringue and put a large spoonful of cream on the base and cover with mixed berries. Sandwich with another meringue and set aside. Repeat with all the meringues and all the cream. Serve immediately. The meringues will keep, without the added cream, in an airtight container for up to one week.

Spiced Baked Apples

Serves 4

6 large dessert apples
75g unsalted butter, softened
50g light brown soft sugar
40g fresh white breadcrumbs
1 green cardamom pod
½ teaspoon ground cinnamon
¼ teaspoon freshly grated nutmeg
Pinch of saffron strands
Finely grated zest of ½ lemon
25g sultanas
25g shelled and chopped pistachio
   nuts
300ml dry cider
Cold pouring cream, to serve

1 Preheat the oven to 200°C/400°F/Gas mark 6. Core the apples leaving them whole. Using a small sharp knife, make a horizontal cut around the middle of the apples – this will prevent the skin from bursting during cooking.

2 Cream the butter, sugar and breadcrumbs together in a medium mixing bowl. Crush the cardamom pods and remove the black seeds. Crush these using a mortar and pestle or with the back of a spoon. Add to the butter mixture along with the cinnamon, nutmeg, saffron and lemon zest. Mix everything together well. Stir in the sultanas and pistachio nuts.

3 Divide this mixture among the 6 apples, stuffing it down tightly into where the cores used to be and piling any excess mixture on top of the apples. Transfer the apples to a ceramic or glass ovenproof dish large enough to hold them all with a little space in between. Pour the cider around the apples.

4 Transfer the dish to the preheated oven and bake for about 40-45 minutes until the apples are very tender.

5 Serve warm with the juices from the baking dish and some cold pouring cream.

Sticky Toffee Pudding

Serves 2

50g butter, softened, plus extra
   for greasing
50g brown sugar
1 egg, beaten
100g self-raising flour
55g chopped dates
2 tablespoons milk

For the sauce
75g brown sugar
125ml double cream
50g butter

Tip

This pudding is ideal
served with mascarpone
or crème fraîche. Try
substituting vanilla-
flavoured prunes for
the dates.

1 Grease a 1¾ pint pudding bowl. Beat the butter and sugar together in a bowl until light and fluffy, then beat in the egg a little at a time. Fold in the flour, then stir in the dates and enough of the milk to give the mixture a soft, dropping consistency.

2 Spoon the mixture into the prepared bowl. Cut a round of greaseproof paper and a round of foil about 5cm larger than the top of the bowl, and grease the bottom of the paper. Put both over the bowl and secure with string.

3 Put the bowl in a large saucepan and pour enough boiling water around the bowl, to come two-thirds of the way up the sides. Cover and simmer for 1–1½ hours until risen and springy when pressed. Check the water occasionally, topping up if necessary.

4 Put all the sauce ingredients in a small saucepan and heat gently, stirring, until combined. Simmer for 5 minutes, or until thickened. Turn the pudding out on to a plate and serve with the sauce.

New England Blueberry Pancakes

Serves 4–6

150g plain flour
½ teaspoon baking powder
½ teaspoon bicarbonate of soda
¼ teaspoon salt
250ml buttermilk
185ml milk
1 tablespoon sugar or honey
25g butter, melted
½ teaspoon vanilla extract
120g fresh blueberries
Melted butter or vegetable oil, for
   frying
Butter and maple syrup or honey,
   to serve

1 Combine the flour, baking powder, bicarbonate of soda and salt in a bowl and make a well in the middle.

2 Whisk the buttermilk, about 125ml of the milk, the sugar or honey, melted butter and vanilla extract together in another bowl. Pour into the well and, using a whisk or fork, stir gently until just combined with the dry mixture. If the batter is too thick, add a little more milk so that is can be poured. Do not overbeat – a few floury lumps do not matter. Gently fold in the blueberries.

3 Heat a large frying pan or pancake griddle (preferably non-stick) over a medium heat and brush with melted butter or vegetable oil. Drop the batter in small ladlefuls on to the hot surface and cook until the edges are set and the surface bubbles begin to break, about 1 minute.

4 Turn each pancake and cook until just golden underneath, about 30 seconds longer. Transfer to a baking tray and keep warm in a low oven until all the batter is cooked. Serve hot with butter and maple syrup or honey.

Double-crust Apple Pie

Serves 6–8

900g cooking apples, peeled,
  cored and sliced
1 tablespoon lemon juice
225g sugar, plus extra for
  sprinkling
2 tablespoons plain flour
½–1 teaspoon ground cinnamon
Freshly grated nutmeg, to taste
15g butter, for dotting
Vanilla ice cream, to serve (optional)

For the pastry
225g plain flour, sifted, plus extra
  for dusting
1 teaspoon sugar
½ teaspoon salt
120g unsalted butter, cut into pieces,
  plus extra for greasing
45g white vegetable fat, chilled
1 egg yolk
1 tablespoon lemon juice
4–6 tablespoons ice water
1 egg, lightly beaten, for glazing

1 To make the pastry, put the flour, sugar and salt into a food processor and pulse once or twice to blend. Sprinkle in the butter pieces and vegetable fat and process for about 10 seconds until the mixture resembles coarse crumbs.

2 With the machine running, add the egg yolk, lemon juice and the water little by little, until the dough begins to come together. Do not allow the dough to form a ball around the blade or it will be tough. Press a little of the dough between your thumb and forefinger; if it does not hold together, add a little more water.

3 Remove the dough and divide it in half. Flatten the pieces into rounds and wrap each in cling film, then chill for 1-2 hours. Leave to soften slightly at room temperature before rolling.

4 Preheat the oven to 220°C/425°F/Gas mark 7. Lightly grease a 23cm pie plate. Put the apples in a large bowl as they are prepared and sprinkle with the lemon juice and toss gently to combine. Mix the sugar, flour, cinnamon and some freshly grated nutmeg together in a small bowl until combined. Sprinkle over the apples and toss to coat the fruit, then set aside.

5 Unwrap one dough round and place on a lightly floured surface. Roll out the dough from the middle towards the edge, turning it by a quarter turn as you roll to keep it in a round shape. The

dough should be about 3mm thick. Gently ease the dough into the pie plate, pressing it in gently. Trim the excess, leaving 1cm overlapping the edge. Brush the edge of the pastry with water and spoon the filling into the pie, mounding it slightly, then dot evenly with the butter.

6 Roll out the second dough round as before and place over the filling. With a sharp knife, cut a few slashes into the top to allow steam to escape. Trim the edge of the dough cover to the rim of the pie plate and turn the overhanging dough underneath up over the edge. Press to seal and crimp the edge. Brush with beaten egg. If you like, re-roll the trimmings and cut decorative leaves and fruits. Arrange on the pie and glaze again. Sprinkle with a little sugar.

7 Bake for about 25 minutes. Cover the edges of the pie with strips of foil to prevent them from over-browning and continue to bake for 20–25 minutes longer until the crust is set and golden and the filling is tender and bubbling.

8 Leave the pie to cool for at least 30 minutes before serving. Serve with vanilla ice cream.

Lychees
with Orange & Ginger

Serves 4

100g sugar
300ml water
2 oranges
16 lychees, peeled and stoned
2 pieces drained stem ginger, sliced
2 passion fruit

1 Heat the sugar and water in a small saucepan, stirring until the sugar has dissolved, then boil the syrup for 1 minute without stirring.

2 Pour the syrup into a serving bowl, and leave until cold. Peel the oranges and segment them, working over the bowl of syrup so that any juice is incorporated. Add the orange segments to the bowl with the lychees and ginger. Stir lightly to combine the ingredients.

3 Spoon into individual glass dishes. Cut the passion fruit in half and scoop the pulp over the fruit. Serve at once.

Chocolate Fondue

Serves 4

375ml double cream
250ml milk
225g plain dark chocolate, roughly
   chopped
Marshmallows, strawberries, chopped
   bananas, cubes of brioche, dates, for
   dipping

1 Pour the cream and milk into a saucepan or fondue bowl and bring to the boil. Turn off the heat and add the chocolate. Stir until the chocolate has melted and the mixture is completely smooth.

2 Serve the chocolate warm with a selection of marshmallows, fruits and brioche.

Tip
When melting chocolate, always break it into small pieces so that it melts evenly. If you are melting chocolate by itself, never melt it over direct heat – place it in a heat-proof bowl over a pan of hot water.

Chocolate Mousse

Serves 8

200g plain dark chocolate, 50 per cent
cocoa solids
4 eggs, separated
175ml double cream, plus extra to
serve

1 Break the chocolate into pieces in a small,
heatproof bowl. Put the bowl over a saucepan
of barely simmering water, ensuring that the bowl
doesn't touch the water, and leave without stirring
until the chocolate has melted. Remove from the
heat and leave to cool for a few minutes.

2 Add 4 egg yolks and beat into the chocolate – it
will thicken the mixture but not stiffen. If the
mixture seems dry and stiff, the chocolate has been
over-heated and you will need to start again.

3 Leave the chocolate mixture to cool for about
15 minutes.

4 Whisk the double cream until it holds soft
peaks. Fold this into the chocolate.

5 Whisk 4 egg whites in a clean bowl until soft
peaks form and fold into the chocolate
mixture. Spoon into 8 small serving dishes, cover
with cling film and chill for about 2 hours before
serving, with a little extra cream if desired.

Chilled Mandarin

& Lemon Mousse

Makes 6 small glasses

Grated zest and juice of 1 lemon
Grated zest of 2 mandarins and the
  juice of 4 mandarins
1 sachet powdered gelatine
4 eggs, separated
100g caster sugar
300ml double cream

To decorate
Whipped cream
Pared lemon and mandarin zest

NOTE: *Recipes using raw eggs should be avoided by infants, the elderly, pregnant women and anyone with a compromised immune system.*

1 Put the fruit zest in a bowl. Measure the fruit juice – it should be no more than 250ml. Pour the measured juice into a small saucepan and sprinkle the gelatine in. Leave to soak for 5 minutes, then heat gently without boiling until the gelatine has dissolved. Leave to cool.

2 Add the egg yolks and sugar to the fruit zest and whisk until the mixture is thick and creamy.

3 With clean beaters, whisk the egg whites in a clean bowl until stiff and whip the cream in another bowl until it forms soft peaks. Gently whisk the gelatine mixture into the yolks, then fold in the cream and finally the egg whites.

4 Spoon the mixture into glasses and chill for 3-4 hours until set. Decorate with whipped cream and lemon and mandarin zest.

Baked Alaska

Birthday Cake

Serves 6

20cm soft sponge flan case
350g raspberry jam
225g raspberries
4 egg whites
225g granulated sugar
8 scoops vanilla or your favourite ice
  cream
Candles or sparklers, to decorate

1 Preheat the oven to 220°C/425°F/Gas Mark 7.

2 Spread the bottom of the flan case with the jam and arrange the raspberries on top.

3 Put the egg whites in a large clean bowl and whisk until stiff peaks form. Beat in the sugar, a spoonful at a time.

4 Put scoops of ice cream over the raspberries to cover. Spread the meringue mixture over the ice cream and sides of the sponge so everything is covered.

5 Bake in the oven for 8–10 minutes. Remove from the oven, decorate with birthday candles or sparklers and serve immediately.

Apple Sauce Sundae

Serves 4

675g cooking apples, peel, cored and
   chopped
60ml water
150g sugar
100g butter
150g fresh brown or rye breadcrumbs
8 tablespoons redcurrant jelly
120ml double cream

Tip
You can add almost
anything to a sundae.
Try sprinkling flaked
almonds, chopped or
mini marshmallows
on top.

1 Put the apples in a heavy-based saucepan with the water. Cover and cook over a medium heat until the apples are very soft, stirring frequently. Process them in a blender or food processor. Stir in 6 tablespoons of the sugar and leave until cold.

2 Melt the butter in a large frying pan. Add the breadcrumbs and remaining sugar and cook over a low heat, shaking the pan frequently, until the crumbs have absorbed the butter and become crisp. Set the pan aside.

3 Warm the redcurrant jelly if necessary, so that it can be spooned. Layer the apple purée, jelly, and browned crumbs in 4 wine glasses, keeping back a little of the jelly for the decoration. Whip the cream until soft peaks form, then swirl it on top of each dessert. Drizzle the remaining redcurrant jelly over the cream and serve.

Chocolate-chip Muffins

Makes 10

400g plain flour
25g unsweetened cocoa powder
1 tablespoon baking powder
½ teaspoon salt
75g caster sugar
120g plain chocolate chips
2 eggs
125ml sunflower or light vegetable oil
250ml milk
1 teaspoon vanilla extract

1 Preheat the oven to 200°C/400°F/Gas mark 6. Line 10 muffin tin cups with double paper liners. Sift the flour, cocoa powder, baking powder and salt into a bowl. Sift again, then stir in the sugar and chocolate chips. Make a well in the middle.

2 Beat the eggs with the oil in another bowl until foamy. Gradually beat in the milk and vanilla extract. Pour into the well in the flour mixture, and stir until just combined.

3 Spoon the mixture into the paper liners. Bake for about 20 minutes until risen, well browned and spongy. Leave to stand for about 10 minutes, then transfer to a wire rack to cool. Serve at room temperature.

Chocolate-covered

Doughnuts

Makes 8

300g plain flour
7g rapid-rise dried yeast
Pinch of salt
50g sugar
2 tablespoons butter, plus extra for
   greasing
150ml milk
2 egg yolks
Vegetable oil, for deep frying
50g plain dark or milk chocolate,
   broken into pieces
Chocolate sprinkles, to decorate

1 Mix the flour in a bowl with the yeast and salt. Add the sugar, then rub in the butter until the mixture resembles fine breadcrumbs.

2 Heat the milk in a saucepan until it is warm, then whisk in the egg yolks. Add the liquid to the flour mixture and mix to a soft dough. Cover with cling film and leave in a warm place for 1 hour to prove until the dough has doubled in bulk.

3 Grease a baking tray. Knock back the dough and knead for 5–10 minutes on a well floured surface. Roll out the dough until 1cm thick, and stamp out rounds with a plain pastry cutter. Make a hole in the middle of each round with your finger. Put the doughnuts on the prepared baking tray and leave to rise for at least 40 minutes until it has doubled in size.

4 Heat the oil for deep-frying in a large deep saucepan to 190°C/375°F. Deep-fry the doughnuts one at a time for about 5 minutes, or until they are golden brown. Drain on kitchen paper and leave to cool.

5 Put the chocolate in a heatproof bowl set over a saucepan of simmering water. Heat until it has melted, then remove from the heat. Leave to cool slightly. Dip the rounded tops of the doughnuts in the melted chocolate, decorate with chocolate sprinkles and leave to set.

Peanut Butter Brownies

Makes 12–16

175g plain dark chocolate
225g butter
450g sugar
4 eggs, lightly beaten
2 teaspoons vanilla extract
50g plain flour
½ teaspoon salt
175g plain chocolate chips

For the peanut butter layer
275g smooth peanut butter
120g butter, softened
30–60g icing sugar, plus extra for
    dusting
175g honey roasted peanuts or white
    chocolate chips

1 Mould a piece of aluminium foil over the bottom of a 20cm square baking tin, pressing it into the corners and smoothing it out evenly.

2 Melt the chocolate and butter in a saucepan over a medium-low heat, stirring frequently, until smooth. Remove from the heat and add the sugar, then stir until the sugar dissolves. Beat in the eggs, then stir in the vanilla extract, flour, salt and chocolate chips until just blended.

3 Spoon half the mixture into the tin and spread evenly into the corners. Freeze for 20 minutes until the surface is firm. Cover the remaining mixture and set aside at room temperature.

4 Preheat the oven to 180°C/350°F/Gas mark 4. Put the peanut butter and butter in a large bowl and, using a hand-held electric mixer, beat for about 2 minutes until smooth and creamy. Beat in the icing sugar and peanuts or white chocolate chips. Drip tablespoonfuls of the peanut mixture over the chocolate layer, then gently spread it evenly to make a smooth layer. Cover with the remaining chocolate mixture in the same way.

5 Bake for 35 minutes, or until the surface is set. Leave the mixture in the tin to cool. Dust with a little icing sugar before cutting into squares or bars.

Apple Cake Bars

Serves 10–12

325g butter, plus extra for greasing

350g tart cooking apples, peeled, cored and thinly sliced

Juice of ½ lemon

325g sugar

450g plain flour, sifted

3 tablespoons baking powder

1½ teaspoons ground cinnamon

Grated zest of 1 lemon

6 eggs, beaten

3 tablespoons milk

For the topping

2 tablespoons demerera sugar

½ teaspoon ground cinnamon

6 tablespoons apricot jam, melted, to glaze

1 Preheat the oven to 180°C/350°F/Gas mark 4. Grease a 33 x 23 x 5cm cake tin and base line with greaseproof paper.

2 Toss the apple slices in the lemon juice. Cream the butter and sugar in a large mixing bowl until pale and fluffy. Sift in the flour, baking powder and cinnamon. Add the lemon zest, eggs and milk, and beat together until smooth.

3 Spoon half the mixture into the prepared tin. Top with half the apple slices, then the remaining cake mixture.

4 Arrange the remaining apple slices over the top and sprinkle with a mixture of demerara sugar and cinnamon.

5 Bake in the oven for 50–60 minutes until golden and firm to the touch. Leave to cool in the tin for 10 minutes them remove to a wire rack. Brush over the apricot jam, then leave to cool completely. Cut into bars to serve.

Cherry Clafoutis

Serves 4

4 tablespoons butter, melted, plus extra
for greasing

2 tablespoons icing sugar, plus extra
for dusting

435g sweet cherries, stoned

115g self-raising flour

45g ground almonds

2 tablespoons sugar

150ml milk

2 eggs

Tip

Clafoutis is a harvest dish
from Limousin and Auvergne
in France. It is a batter pudding
filled with sweet black cherries
– a substantial ending to a
meal after a hard day in
the fields.

1 Preheat the oven to 190°C/375°F/Gas mark 5.
Grease a 23cm shallow baking dish thoroughly
and dust the bottom with the measured icing sugar.
Arrange the cherries on top.

2 Mix the flour, ground almonds and sugar
together in a bowl. Pour the melted butter into
a jug and whisk in the milk and eggs.

3 Make a well in the centre of the flour mixture
and add the butter mixture. Stir well, gradually
incorporating the flour, to make a smooth batter.

4 Pour the batter over the cherries and bake for
25 minutes. Leave to cool slightly, then dust
with icing sugar. Alternatively, run a knife around
the rim of the dessert and invert it on to a flat
serving platter. The top of the clafoutis (formerly
the bottom) should be creamy and studded with
cherries, while the rest of the mixture should have
set to a sponge. Dust the top with icing sugar.

Boston Cream Pie

Serves 8

Butter, for greasing
5 eggs
150g sugar
150g plain flour

For the filling
4 egg yolks
50g sugar
4 tablespoons cornflour
2 teaspoons vanilla extract
450ml milk
300ml double cream

1 Preheat the oven to 200°C/400°F/Gas mark 6. Grease and line the bases of a 23cm springform cake tin and a 26 x 17cm shallow rectangular tin with greaseproof paper.

2 Put the eggs and sugar in a large heatproof bowl set over a saucepan of barely simmering water, and whisk until the mixture is pale and thick and holds a trail. Remove from the heat and whisk for a further 3-4 minutes, or until very light.

3 Sift the flour over the mixture and carefully fold in with a metal spoon. Spoon a very thin layer of the mixture over the bottom of the rectangular tin to a depth slightly thicker than 5mm. Pour and scrape the rest of the mixture into the round tin.

4 Bake both cakes for 12-15 minutes, or until light golden and firm; the cakes should spring back when lightly pressed with a finger. Leave to cool in the tins for 5 minutes, then turn out on to wire racks.

5 To make the filling, beat the egg yolks, sugar, cornflour, vanilla extract and 2 tablespoons milk together in a bowl. Heat the remaining milk in a saucepan to boiling point. Pour over the egg mixture, beating, then return to the pan and heat gently, stirring until thickened, but do not boil. Pour back into the bowl and cover with a piece of damp greaseproof paper. Leave to cool.

6 Cut the round sponge horizontally into two layers and fit one back into the cleaned tin, cut side up. Trim the edges from the rectangular sponge, then cut into 3cm wide strips. Fit these around the side of the tin to make a shell.

7 Whip the cream in a chilled bowl until thick. Stir the cooled custard, and then fold in the cream. Pour into the sponge shell. Lay the second sponge on top, cut side up. Chill in the refrigerator overnight before serving.

Stove-top Rice Pudding
with Dried Fruit

Serves 4–6

1 litre milk
140g dried cherries, dried cranberries, raisins or sultanas, or a mixture
3–4 strips orange zest
1 cinnamon stick
225g short-grain rice, such as pudding rice or risotto rice
250ml double cream
120g sugar
1 teaspoon vanilla extract
¼ teaspoon salt
Cinnamon sugar, brown sugar or maple syrup, to serve
Whipped cream (optional)

Tip

It's best to use short grain rice for puddings and rice desserts as the grains swell and absorb the liquid to give a creamy consistency.

1 Put the milk, dried fruit, orange zest and the cinnamon stick in a large, heavy-based saucepan and set over a medium heat. Bring to a simmer and stir in the rice.

2 Reduce the heat to low and cook, stirring frequently to avoid scorching, for about 20 minutes, or until the rice is tender and the mixture creamy.

3 Stir in the cream, sugar, vanilla extract and salt and continue cooking for about 10 minutes longer, until the rice is completely tender and the mixture thick and creamy.

4 Pour the rice pudding into a large bowl and leave to cool to room temperature, stirring occasionally. Sprinkle with cinnamon sugar or brown sugar, or drizzle with maple syrup and serve with whipped cream, if using.

Summer Berry

Shortcakes

Makes 8

675g fresh ripe strawberries and other
    summer berries, hulled and sliced
2–3 tablespoons caster sugar
1–2 tablespoons raspberry juice or
    1 tablespoon orange juice
90g butter, diced, plus extra for
    greasing
225g plain flour, plus extra for dusting
2½ teaspoons baking powder
½ teaspoon salt
2 tablespoons sugar, plus extra for
    sprinkling
250ml double or whipping cream,
    whipped to soft peaks
Icing sugar, for dusting
Fresh mint leaves, to decorate

1 Put the berries in a large bowl and toss with the caster sugar and fruit juice. Leave to stand until the juices begin to run, stirring occasionally.

2 Preheat the oven to 220°C/425°F/Gas mark 7 and grease a baking sheet. Stir the flour, baking powder, salt and sugar together in a large bowl. Add the butter and, using a pastry blender or your fingertips, run it into the flour mixture until coarse crumbs form. Using a fork, lightly stir in all but 1 tablespoon of the cream, little by little, to make a soft dough.

3 Turn the dough out on to a lightly floured work surface and knead 6-8 times, until smooth. Pat or roll the dough into a rectangle about 1cm thick. Using a round cutter, stamp out 8 rounds or, if you prefer, cut into 8 x 7.5cm squares. Arrange 7.5cm apart on the baking sheet. Brush the tops with the remaining cream and sprinkle with sugar.

4 Bake for about 10 minutes until set and the tops are pale golden. Transfer the shortcakes to a wire rack to cool.

5 Using a fork or serrated knife, split the shortcakes in half horizontally. Put the bottoms on 8 desserts plates and spoon the chilled whipped cream over them. Spoon over the berries. Put the shortcake tops on the berries and dust the shortcakes with icing sugar.

Menu Ideas

Brunch

Chakchouka (p.129)
New England Blueberry Pancakes (p.226)

Grilled Cheese & Tomato Sandwiches
   with Bacon (p.54)
Green Bean & Mozzarella Salad (p.201)
Chocolate-chip Muffins (p.237)

Parsley & Leek Frittata (p.135)
Chocolate-covered Doughnuts (p.238)

Eggs Benedict (p.134)
Tropical Fruit Salad (p.221)

Lunch

Quick Mushroom Carbonara (p.59)
Apple Cake Bars (p.241)

Easy Burritos (p.75)
Berry Ice Lollies (p.214)

Bacon Cheeseburgers (p.68)
Chickpea & Tomato Salad (p.195)

Fish Finger Sandwiches
   with Mayonnaise (p.117)
Apple Sauce Sundae (p.236)

Chow Mein with Mangetout (p.153)
Broad Beans with Prosciutto (p.108)

Italian Submarine Sandwiches (p.55)
Chilled Mandarin & Lemon Mousse (p.233)

New Potato & Crispy Bacon Salad (p.56)
Courgette Bread (p.208)

Grapefruit, Prawn & Avocado Salad (p. 102)
Stove-top Rice Pudding with Dried Fruit
    (p.245)

Dinner Party Buffet

Chef's Salad (p.197)
Provençal Ratatouille (p.155)
Onion Quiche (p.139)
Tuna Melts (p.113)
New England Fishballs (p.120)
Peanut Butter Brownies (p.240)

Barbecue

Kansas City Pork Ribs (p.67)
Spicy Chicken Kebabs (p.20)
Grilled Tuna with Warm Bean Salad (p.114)
Grilled Corn Cobs with
    Flavoured Butter (p.174)
Tropical Fruit Salad (p.221)

Dinner Party

New England Clam Chowder (p.94)
Roast Rib of Beef with
    Caramelized Shallots (p.76)
Duchesse Potatoes (p.166)
Cherry Clafoutis (p.243)

Smoked Trout Terrine
    with Cucumber Salad (p.121)
Traditional Roast Chicken (p.34)
Luxury Mashed Potatoes (p.166)
Succotash (p.173)
Double-crust Apple Pie (p.228)

Home-smoked Salmon (p.92)
New England Potato Salad (p.172)
Beef & Onion Pies (p.70)
Brussels Sprouts
    with Sweet Potatoes (p.183)
Spiced Baked Apples (p.224)

Celebration Meal

Crab Louis (p.97)
Poached Whole Salmon (p.105)
Hot Vegetable Salad (p.184)
Baked Alaska Birthday Cake (p.235)

Caesar Salad (p.194)
Baked Country Ham (p.66)
Maple-baked Acorn Squash (p.189)
Latkes (p.171)
Boston Cream Pie (p.244)

Cheese Soufflé (p.131)
Roast Turkey with Sausage
    & Sage Stuffing (p.46)
Sweet Potato Casserole
    with Marshmallow Topping (p.176)
Carrots with Maple Syrup (p.182)
Pumpkin Pie (p.220)

Marinated Prawns
    with Dill Mayonnaise (p.104)
Braised Lamb Shanks
    with Mirepoix Vegetables (p.80)
Leek & Potato Layer (p.169)
Sticky Toffee Pudding (p.225)

Dinner

Rice Vermicelli with Pork & Vegetables
    (p.63)
Braised Sugar Snaps with Lettuce (p.178)
Lychees with Orange & Ginger (p.229)

Patatas Bravas (p.167)
Spanish Pork with Tomatoes
    & Chorizo (p.64)
Spiced Courgettes (p.185)
Caramel Ice Cream (p.217)

Old-fashioned Meatloaf (p.78)
Potato Pancakes with Creamy Mushrooms
    (p.156)
Chocolate Mousse (p.232)

Roast Cod with Fried Gremolata
    Breadcrumbs (p.119)
Pumpkin Couscous (p.146)
Chilled Mandarin & Lemon Mousse
(p.233)

Honey-orange Chicken (p.32)
Risotto Primavera (p.142)
Mango Ice Cream (p.216)

Vegetarian Dinner

Roast Vegetable Lasagne (p.143)
Green Bean & Mozzarella Salad (p.201)
Poached Pears with Maple Syrup & Pecans
    (p.218)

Children's Sleepover Party

Warm Cheese & Smoked Chilli Dip
    with Tortilla Chips (p.163)
Cheese & Tomato Pizza (p.127)
Southern Fried Chicken (p.24)
Panzanella (p.198)
Chocolate Fondue (p.230)

Picnic

Tortilla Wraps with Honey Roast Ham
    & Pepper Slaw (p.52)
Chicken Satay Skewers
    with Sweet Chilli Sauce (p.23)
Classic Healthy Coleslaw (p.191)
Waldorf Salad (p.196)
Summer Berry Shortcakes (p.246)

Index